ABOUT THE BOOK

Welcome everybody to a truly splendid and aptly titled book. "Triumphs or T
This book literally ensures you to be filled with rhyme and reason of some really wild poetry. Honest. "Triumphs or Tragedies" has excellent rhyming poems ranging from humanism to faith to fantasy and how about it be topped off with a little fiction. Poems inside these vaults of victory are bound to make you think deep. Real deep.

They will also make you look within, strike a harmonious chord, and even possibly stray from sin. Please forgive me, for I consider myself to not get to weighed in or down without the essence of change. A way to rearrange-Through the ego, body, soul, and mind. A way to emotionally find-what makes us not only smile, yet cling to that smile. For a long, long while . How about infinitely! Next on deck as a figure of speech, is focusing on all of our good memories. And better yet! How much good time is left to be found and had. How much is still within reach. Not to preach-yet I believe in God and Christ. Which some of this book also does consist of, the ability to resurrect and fly like a dove. I cannot deny this book although also covers poems that are sad, some that are downright mad, some are glad, and the rest of the book is, well, iron clad. I hope that you truly love this book and remember

that all of this poetry goes out there for you. May God bless-Oh-check out my first book- "Intricate Emotion: downside of discursiveness" which is sold through AuthorHouse! Once again, thanks and enjoy!

Sincerely yours,
Brian Moilanen

2015—

I WISH You ALL

THE BEST!

LOVE,

Brian Moilanen

<u>Credits</u>

The process of compiling and putting together well established credits is not any easy task! I will inform you that this assignment is usually increasingly tedious and long-but I am going to keep it brief and exactly to the point. Okay, well here goes. I want to thank Jehovah God for a mind full of entertaining thought with idea. My only aide in this was primarily a dictionary and a thesaurus. Also on just a few poems I conferred with my Holy Bible. Now for my main credits that come to mind. I thank Jehovah God for direction which is overshadowed within love and unity. Next on deck I thank these holy angels of Jehovah God that promote a good spiritual foundation for helping me out with almost everything that life brings to us humans on this sometimes chaotic and trying world. Next up-I give thanks to my immediate family and to all of my friends. You know who you are! God bless us one and all. Thanks a million. See you all soon.

Cordially yours,

Brian Moilanen

2nd Class Citizen

Treat me
As if I were you-henceforth you would want to be pleased
So what is it like to live the American dream
Like my poverty struggling friends-we have only been teased
Poignantly speaking-do I truly even exist
Yes-Yet only when problems protest
Mental conflicts resides within my stubborn soul
For if someone else is throwing my dice
Won't you at least let me see them role
My brain contends with my flesh-I will firmly attest
If I am a priests claim-one that is exonerated and blessed
Then why is this innocent mind-Put through this yet self conjured- a mental arrest
Sometimes
Occasionally
Blurring this life within a day-is more than a hint to me yet only wanting more
Do my homework and not forget to read the good book
Dirt poor yet sinning and still jealous of those I could overcome-so much too explore
On the way out
Breeze amongst the window-yet please firmly shut the door
Education-I do have quite a bit
Yet now my dreams strangely defy money-I want beach sand and an ocean's shore
A new beginning
Re-begin this record yet at a different part
My rules now
Yet again-please remember it is if gold and silver-a precious heart
I have been spit at
Shoved conveniently to the side
But I keep the past in today's mind
No thumbs up needed to acquire a ride
I have given
Almost all that I once did own
And this world has readily taken
The good that you have collected from me-on the face of you- it is shown
One way to keep this train rolling-is that inward I have grown
Is it that this big red heart has made its way known
Trying hard to create remedy
So darn much with my life's story-more than you is what I abundantly see
So don't run-don't flee
Could I for a moment
Live inside of you
Although bruised-I am not broken
Entertaining a dream is what I confirm-and shall do
King of ration
Stretch a dime
For near that of a...week
This man without ample money despite
By way of evil-has never been took

WRITTEN BY: Brian Moilanen 2013

A Hand to Hold

Obviously once again the daily pressures build
Yet on the other hand I do speak with fulfillment of wish
Have any of your dreams been complete and sustained
Unconditional loves eventually strives to understand all
Are you unfairly pained
And through the process of danger-ready to take a fall
Is touching base concerned with my need to manifest affection
And in fashion-by keeping the sane continuous and enduring
Love does although seek kind attraction
Yet is this the simplicity that is contagious or even alluring
And for the matter-does love know all that portray
To earnestly seek and find
Not delusion or methodology-I know the way
Touching base with a foreshadowed unique sense
Do you see what I see and ascribe to what I play
Steps or procedures
Caught within a maze I squirm
Like a fish out of water
That won at his attempt to secure the baited worm
A hand to hold
Demonstrating a sure fire way
Leading by and with relation of example
Hoarding up on life's joys
Go large-and subscribe to what is beyond ample
Brisk summer time walks in the park
A Friday night at the Sweet Heart drive inn
A merciful onslaught of yesteryear
Now that is my remark which I do embark
A hand to hold
An open wallet with sufficient cash-How else to be bold
Do not scold or challenge
For even though young at heart-I understand we won't break this mold

WRITTEN BY: Brian Moilanen 2013

A Party Somewhere

Somewhere in this suppressed sleepy city
Lies a bash of a party linked to a wild destination
My brain playing tricks and is lethargic with foist
Necessity of a self medicated prescription of fun allowing for proclamation
Yell it-scream it-let all hear your desire
With the pain intact evolves the insane
Do not flush this energy down the drain
Prophetic-Neurotic-exotic
Carnal eyed vision surfaces seldom- yet now is prevalent
Yet not disturbed –Just a taste of the problematic
Frolic and frugality
How can I earn some type of substance in a bland land
Dreams of ocean-equipped with the sand
Advocate for jollity
I think I'll hit a home run with an equation of neutrality
A party somewhere
Currently in my own world churning manifesto
An altered world within reach
Snap fingers-do an absolution and proceed with saying presto
Tonight thus far is a happening go
I have currently just had my 4th cup of hot black joe
And glance in solace desperation at my crucifix
I am entitled to a good time
Redeeming grace
Common place
Restless souls-how many miles to urban society
I think I need a woman blessed with sanctum
To set my restlessness at a mild form of ease
Polite of course
Pass me a cold one-Oh did I say please
Somehow driving these city streets
After an hour and a half
Alone with God, self, soul and me
I find a party on crossroads Stuart and Bernard
My eyes accompany a host of hosts
Half of the inside jamming house and half smother the yard
Beautiful egos
Timid souls
Attraction testing soul and spirit
The music cranks at climatic sound wave
So loud it could wake even those at rest within the grave
Smoke fills the air
Slowly finding its way to the lungs
Green gathers in
Righteous heart ponders and violates sin
Yet it is curious of what surrounds
I look within and a victor is what abounds
I feel good
And good feels me
Tree limbs represent arms of comfort and speculum
Some at this here representation are grand souls
Just a soldier
Yet only the most splendid understand the fun time role
Have a comforting drink
And while at it-enjoy a smoke
A life-time of demands
Should also see humility-and locate even the underside of a joke

WRITTEN BY: BRIAN MOILANEN-2010

A World's Nightmare

Agnostics
Evolutionists
Freethinkers
Unbelievers
Eat your heart out
Then save some for your fellow foe
Another John Doe just died
And wears medically a new labeled tag upon his toe
World's population drops day by day
Grim reality is quickly growing-despite the prospering fields of wheat and corn
Grips of mankind faltering and failing-how to possibly allocate for futures way
Churches decline in growth, belief and hope
Theft, disease and famine raise the roof
As the witnessing crowd of religion embraces the Pope
What will happen to a depressed colonizing planet
How and what to measure
The shovels have dug
Only to find the number zero is the treasure
The planets are not in line-off course and guiding towards a ruptured bug
Computers rarely work
And world leaders have a serious tone
I just spoke with many clergies over the telephone
No devils to intervene or confuse with terror
Yet I must add
No angels either or just to assist in love
Buckle your seat belts
For what appears as a visionaries view of death with cataclysmic suicide
No more black holes
No more light phenomena
No more anything is totally near
Just observe these words to hear what they say
Death of mother earth
The end of all galaxies
Black holes
Comets
Planets
Moons and stars
And the same as is such
People drop dead at the sight of the Sun
Survivors just hobble with crutch
Because primarily there is no where to run
Darkness vastly entertains the miniscule light
Yet seemingly it always does evade
The final feature-An end of world parade
For something not yet seen- yet recorded and written this fateful day
And if there was readers of this
They would break down and fathom within utter dismay
What was left of yesterday
Just merely corrodes into grotesque decay

WRITTEN BY: BRIAN MOILANEN 2010

Absolution

This word with theory or definition is able to change
Does it mean perfect-while it is whole and complete
Yet it is subject to its external range
Or is it not
Not limited at all
And in its valediction-It says goodbye with firm love secured
A Hush hush and not a fall
Do you see beneath what is obscured
What has helped the conscience brain move onward
And not backward
Do you see both the young and elderly cured
Okay-maybe cured is to elusive of a word to use
Yet absolution and its forming elements of properties won't get blurred
Only seen forthright before it is understood
And that creates a righteous platform
One that of a hierarchy of events should only conceive as ...good
Another term of this word is absolution and is according to and with
No expressed object or objects
This usually ties in with verbs and its transitive
Also known as being transitional-or rare meaning of a verb
Such as-the car tires mangle treacherously around the seemingly treacherous rotating curb
A pivotal word
With definition of may and much
Yet do your studying now
And absolution usually leaves you complete
So do not have a cow
Should I also mention absolution can mean pureness-
Without the mixing of sin or whatsoever anything else
If you have a good heart in direct portion to this poem
Check your juggler artery on your neck near your head
And see if the blood flow continues to freely roam
Forgive me if I momentarily jump off the subject at hand
For I understand this audience is my boss
And that they are in ingenuously the ones in command
Forgiveness
Do not forget about forgetting
To complete this salutation
You must first understand-life is too short to consort to only regretting
And pray if you will for others
Include the self
Yet not the self as the first lead-in your prayer of event or events
And when driving-no horseplay
2000 pounds shall keep you on the roadway as it only cements
Now speaking in philosophy-
Absolution is that which is thought of as existing in and by itself
Without relation to anything else
Now that is both exciting and nerve-racking
Even though ordained-does that not give you the chills

WRITTEN BY: BRIAN MOILANEN 2010

Analysis of My Ego

An ongoing analysis of my valid ego
To the slim crowd of leaders-such as I
If I were half crazy-how much of it would split and in vestige show
And to that may I add up
When my temperament appears upbeat-is it truth to that daring statement
Or is it merely a sense of falsified glad
Can we actually judge ourselves between
And amongst our own personified ideas
And also….
When does the spark igniting the wick get inspected-then accordingly lit
Ego means the self thinking-feeling-and acting
Distinct from the external world
Yet what we created we fathom and also
What we greatly admire-such as a flag-what has been furled
Now….and yes now
I can speak conscience to soul privately
Covertly and furtive
In solemn and sincere regard
The United States flag I console and keep
As it is not tarnished, soiled or blatantly charred
Misfortunes
Certain ones to a degree-
Everyone does have or own
Just one of me in this world is sufficient
Side-winding I might just be-that is if I had a clone
Rejection
Subjection
Both of which I have often unfairly felt
Oppression
At times I have slowed down and disdainfully forced to wear out
Yet I always put back in
Wherever there is charity or case of somebody's immediate need
Moreover to religion-faith-or even ones creed
Both substances occur to humans especially-and mine is to plant a seed
Detection
Human issues of all kind put Christ
As the center and medium of the Godhead
Study-or at least read the holy bible
And translate and read what the apostles once said
And also what was done
All of this sunshine
Yet how many miles are you-yes you-from the warm gentle sun
For it represents joy for most
How about we celebrate-this wine topped off in this challis-will commune our toast
The simplicity of the flavor is quite savory as
Demands for it all to be finished
Remember this is a demand-and not a plea
Is your ego true or false-or and also comprehended by angels
To yourself be true
Then the latter half of this statement-always shines and knows what to do

WRITTEN BY: BRIAN MOILANEN-2010

Another Time Missing You

Vivid pictures and snapshots of you
Clutter a hazy blue bedroom floor
Sailing away are treasured memories
A frigid rolling sea without any nearby shore
Sullen loneliness is knocking at my door again
Pervading another almost lost memory
That somehow still finds its way in
This furtive moment seeks another time
That helplessly finds me missing you again
My remedy despite is passionate rum laden with sweet lime
Never allowing to malice or to become chagrin
Practice makes repetition and the venting of pleasant rhyme
For we are tight and becoming even closer together
Today a day garish with pristine aqua sky
Filling any void is a luminous yellowed sun
Another inclination that always does imply
If you lose your hopes just how to obtain fun
Sorting through my shelf of dreams
Happiness destined-or is this all what it really seems
I need to locate my soul-mate
To which we can live forever and it's infinite tomorrow
A gentle trying release
To omit any ongoing past sorrow

Written by: Brian Moilanen

Are the Days Getting Longer

These days are precious-and only getting much longer
Sad to say regardless of-mightily you although feel weak
Defy myself of this situation-I only feel stronger
Time-it ticks and tocks repetitively
Yet it is on my side-As I am more than ever-ready
Considerably-I watch my every-move
As I approach each footstep solid and steady
At the minimum-you hold and console that stuffed animal bear
That in which you title-as the prized teddy
The kiss of time is intrepid- and yes-well developed
And is not letting loose of its barbaric anchored grip
Surrounded by determination- a scheme that is well enveloped
Do not cheat yourself or….
Get mugged mentally or spiritually of what others take for granted
I adhere to fairness in this sometimes charade of complex that equal life
And see things not as utterly slanted
Pouring of this wine and also elements-exertion without the strife
Was it successfully and properly decanted
I think for myself-with Christ's guiding power
Even if in a game I could sensibly lose
Tail between these legs won't be seen-for I will not persist to the word of cower
Does desire and dream outlive what is freely given from…
The excitement of a new or fresh beginning
Exceptions to understanding-that is where rules are placed
Break free from sinning-and observe the past-as it is gone-erased
Days of long
Peculiarity of even minutes alone do gladly seem
Much more than idle and fruitful-strong
Is the divine intervention of Almighty God
Where peace is foreseen and gainfully acquired
A candid laugh-a loving hug-genuine love
Essentials of this haven-detriments-rules required
Moments-measurements of duration-scope of above
Almost as if in a void
At least in the essence of foible time-only in this creation
Not to respond-in other way
Yet sensitive and excitable-is this the hemispheres new dismay
Nobody has limits or boundaries now-being at the edge
To the United States of America
Is which in what I do pledge
Tight rope walking is also done
100 feet plus from nerve shaking edge to edge
Elongated
Minimal treachery
Just tedious
As you can plainly see
Protracted
Extended
Longer days-And this belongs to all
Focus in this world-then it is tough for even that of a fall

WRITTEN BY: BRIAN MOILANEN 2010

Attached Ways

Attached almost clinging ways
Despite and beside
Intervention of the psyche-the door closes as it plays
Do what it commands and obey what it says
Do not although jounce out on me
I was just beginning to work-yet you walk out on poor desperate me
A slammed door shut-accompanied with inappropriate word
A screaming car from the winds windy front drive
How absurd
Why did you think I was barely half-alive
Your fuse appeared to be lit
And I was with it holding a lit match-and actually set it aflame
Disregard assurance
No one wins as the testified procedure may have its claim
Arguments
Not seeing eye to eye
Your face being a painted picture
A cloyed expression stares back as a sigh
Soured
Grimaced
Not of nature being happy-currently far from pure
Like a traveling rock band
Yet if that were so-would we complete our tour
Although missing you
Quite ubiquitously so
Sweeping away the yesterday
Yet….not really financially raking in the dough
I do have time for you
Even beyond infinity
And yet just what is that
The door now is open in understanding obtaining mostly sweat
A day at a time
Our attached ways create color of all spectrum
You are a calligrapher-and ink the scribe
Hard to let go
Hard to let go even ever
Of the past
Do not become discouraged by not knowing
If our future will hold firm and of sticky substance
I understand your bond with your mother
And know on Sundays-she divinely repents
Reaffirm and re-shine
End that day of monotony
Relinquish it with a strong glass of white wine
Who holds the future
The future is who whom holds the above
I shall close my mental diary now
And focus on sweet-yet sometimes gone sour-love

WRITTEN BY: BRIAN MOILANEN

Bad Luck

Chaos
Disorder
A mess on my hands
Because when bad luck calls
Quickly you learn it compels orders along with demands
I see a grim pity
But as for the eager you
You do not truly sense this
Shattered essence along with condolence
Nerves are growing fragile and weary
And my brainpower stupefied and ultimately dense
I turn away from fellow peers
As a dispirited and misguided glazed moon
Slightly looks back with no more than haunting glares
Precisely string me thru
The tiny needle's thinning eye
Only to find that the thread will only jostle
And often times-to soon break
Guide me along this turmoil of mayhem
Which is circling that of a black snake
Another miniscule number 13
My God given number-beit also my claim
Contradictions
Inflictions
A game seeking victory yet befriended and at a loss
The resume of my life
I watch the tyrants find the garbage can
And my opportunity just gets a toss
Some pray for benedictions
the unspoken word quickly departs
Only another sad ending
Without the most congenial of starts

WRITTEN BY: Brian Moilanen 2013

Become Better or Bitter

I would highly suspect at this moment to detach and ultimately transform
Repair-change-and also to mention I would recommend to modify
Damaged soul-along with a bleeding broken heart
And as for the remainder of me
Is it true-that most of it has been torn derisively apart
Not an attempt to cry or bellyache
Yet look into my unbarred eyes
And you undoubtedly see only refuge- and a product of forsake
Nothing to hide from
I believe and shall say-beware-you might just want to hide from me
I would reckon to mention
I would greatly prefer to be with the rest-that of a gleeful spree
Analyzing and soul searching
I have pondered with that until blue in the face
What has been written in our history books
Was written before our history was even done through action or thought
That is like being just a number
And although-this hand has fought
Yet time and time again
I uncover salvation
And with its terms, turn from sin
Besieged
Empty pockets
A war in my head continues
And yes-I can almost see and hear those screaming rockets
Enough although of this melancholy of truth
Because defiantly the truth may hurt
Destitution of finances my companionship finds only rock bottom
And I speak with altercation of being noisy and overt
My good days versus my bad days
They are running strangely enough
Hand in hand-neck in neck
This old junker of a car I pointedly drive
Resembles an old wreck complacent of being a wreck
Yet it beats walking aimlessly-a piece of material mind keeps me alive
I have figured out despite
A way to win this game of life-that apparently does not sway- speaking ethereal-ever end
Count your blessings
And give to the beggar-and a down and out story he will lend
Maybe I do not have it so bad
Heck-my clothes appear clean and also as polished and forthrightly clad
Now as mentioned before
I must drive on
I must push to the top
Even a silver bullet in my detonated time bomb ticker
Just will not stop me
Only make my unyielding competition-become weaker and sicker
Spiritual warfare
That is what my family claims
Just arbitration's of an undying totalitarian type-friend or foe
Somehow I am sick of the madness
And shall catch a plane and remotely go
They go nearly blind-as I will chasten for all to see
Is this the end to my story of short
A humble proposition to my boss-God-in which I must report

WRITTEN BY: BRIAN MOILANEN-2010

Beyond Love-much Beyond

Intense affection
Feeling dead no longer
Self-resurrection
My expression of my complete attraction
Causes that end more than just physical attraction
Love-the love of genuine
Spirited-the sweetness of wine
A night as tonight-a feeling so divine
All these components-simplified as fine
To be faithful forever
Gladly I would-walk that line
Flowers enlighten this glistening moon
Today's horoscope fulfilled the ultimate sign
Even if tricks or being fathomed with by frolic-I did not invite that host
I would overcome-jump-and do the most
If I had a dictionary-I would read what true love meant to us
Ecstasy derived
Nearing fantasy
Too little of this-could we have ever survived
Geniality
It comforts kindly
A true treat-whether Valentine's day or that or this
A kiss that never ends
Time does not play tricks
Like a prism-it only bends
Beyond love-much beyond
Our love is close despite
Skipping stones at the marveled pristine pond
Your smile-lined with grace and full of pearl white
What a match-probably made in heaven
Beautiful, dainty, and for my eyes-more than delight
Why wait for what the next day does bring
Therapeutic itself
You hit every key exact-joy is to hear you sing
Multiplied satisfaction
It is not my action
I base myself-and us-upon reaction
Or force of nature or merely inquisitiveness
A way to play kindly
A state of love
No disguise needed-only a discreet kiss and tell
If I have ever offended
From my mouth-the words shall not exit-they will be not expelled
Leisure
With you even at work-I feel the same
Or so I claim
With you I am your full time star
And do not need that of an intoxicated crowd
That which usually surrounds the essence of salacious bar

WRITTEN BY: BRIAN MOILANEN-2010

Bring Me Into the Light

How about we bring up a brilliant form of sight
Overshadowed currently only with nearing prestige-concurring with passage
Yet that depends totally on the rising- and its generations of height
Circumstances relate to heredity possibly of common wealth
Yet do not overlook virtues of positive consequence
And where lies the wages of your present leisured health
Responsibility
It is chiefly much-and yet not all of it depends on my complete sole existence
Have you not figured out that the fickle resistance
Adds up to firm yet pliable persistence
He who often cares
Is predominantly the one who wins
Now to shift gears
Is what I will with compassion do
Find God with Christ so to say as chairmen
And these two will show you thru
The doors that are locked
The windows that are fused with metal and constantly shut
Inspired by the nobles best
And to not fall in a rut
As for the wizard of Oz
The tin man is made of tin metal, courage and pins
To bring into the light
Usually gathers from the dark
We all have had the dark in us-and around before
So why not hungrily embark
Catastrophes
The return reaction may be even greater than it is worse
Find time for biblical scripture
And within that time-find a moment to comfortably rehearse
Religion corrupts sin
Much more than I am able to mention
Observe the less fortunate and within others-God of device releases tension
Just whatever may be said of times gone bad
Pacify even further those who are religious
Infringing upon doubt-nobody now will go mad
My brain salutes
To some degree all of those who did successfully accomplish
If bitterness rears its ugly head
Forgive and forget-and follow accordingly to Christian wish
Suggestions
Hints
Words spoken soft and such
Cornered only by others problems
Fortitude is as a friend and is remedied as the strongest crutch
Anticipation
Lives proclamation
Spot those individuals of spiritual worth
Yet I believe it is slightly different than ones credential
Check the map of agendas events-and follow all of the sequential
Is my opposition gone
No-sometimes it always does add to compounding friction
Customary format
That of the truth-We everyday face the same conflict-that of a contradiction
WRITTEN BY: BRIAN MOILANEN-2010

Building God's Earthly House

God's word-God's holy unique message
Both coded-covert-and a shining secret
The law of the land unfortunately-is in man's hands only
Or is it
Let us chronologically go back in time
And have a true heavenly ordained visit
Mankind's laws will take a tremendous blow with powering hit
Some that do not believe will blatantly just
Think and eminently sit
Yet the flip-side makes its bold firm extravagance
The masons under David's son-set forth to build for the Lord
The throne of God's kingdom shall soon be established over Israel
Yet as nearly a new commandment it is mentioned
A project such as this-will not shed blood-as we all understand means not to kill
The Lord will be with thee
And he shall prosper thou
In the eyes of man to your Lord I will say to you
Follow my word now-And take a praised bow
Mankind now is given understanding
Wisdom
And a charged Lord's commanding
Do not neglect to fulfill the statutes and judgments of Moses
Concerning Israel-be strong, of courage, dread not or be dismayed
Then what is our loyal servants final reward…
A house of a hundred thousand talents beit of gold- the same amount
For silver and yes also for brass
Do you not understand listeners of my audience-can you truly even count
This God Almighty-works with utter and divinity at class
Oops …did I forget to mention the iron that has
No weight…timber and stone also to the concluding of this
Time passes quickly
Be cautious-For if you blink your eyes-a piece of the great you just might miss
As David said….Is not the Lord your God with you
And hath he not given you rest on every side
For you see my friend –God on this trip is your pilot
And you as a passenger only must require too enjoy this cathartic ride
Now set your heart and soul to seek the Lord
Your God-to bring the ark of covenant of the Lord
And the holy vessels of God-into the house that is to be built
To the name of the Lord
Now I must and will add that their
Servant crew is mighty-abiding-and strong
The service of the house of the Lord
Whom has mansions in the heavens
And castles displayed abundantly upon the earth
As you know-some were chosen to sanctify
The most of holy things
With incense burned before the Lord
Atonement-peace-and gathering of good and Almighty God
Withdraw from the possible combat-and throw down your sword
After the Lord ministered both then and today
Certain names were blessed forever
Only with God's undying efforts-that are true and resolve in a loving way
WRITTEN BY: Brian Moilanen 2012

Chasing Shadows

This all has been left a split second behind
Chasing accompanying shadows
It is difficult to review and even more than that rewind
Is this a flabbergasting contest
A perpetuating emergency on human interest
A continual pest
Twice bitten –once shy
The means of a harmonizing sounding arrest
Yet I know I must harbor to push and accordingly try
How far
To the galaxy-farther than heaven-yet why
Shadows appear as silhouettes
With contours that shape quicker than the naked eye
All in silence
And without sigh or reply
Or for that matter nothing material left to comply
Simplified
Exemplified
Must find something of which to boast
Look behind
Sneak ahead
Peer underneath what is underneath
Maybe a Christmas carol
That is adorned upon the door-displayed as a wreath
What next
Where to hide
Shadows chase
Is it all dark illusion
Or a mad mans brand new approach
Collusion
Infusion
Mental self -medicating institution
Shadows do not waste
Therefore they are picky-and do not haste
Are you my friend
With hints of a guardian angel
To guard and protect
Always zebra like cover and demonstration
Yet not allowing to ever neglect
At the same time
A second before
Rarity-a split second late
Yet despite these analogies
With the dark veil thou shall not throw me under
The rain
The riveting thunder
All elements of this mostly sane planet
I understand now
That not a thing is ever taken for granted

WRITTEN BY: BRIAN MOILANEN-2010

Chronologically Ordering the Senses!

No not organized-to say ego
No normalized focus-at least in that what I have comprehended
What appears to be sense of psychology
Yours is dormant and jostled-what appears might be apprehended
Premonition
Do not take this as light
Suspicion
Do not forsake-or abandon with humility this moment-in flight
The inclination towards expanding the suitable mind
Sometimes introverts within the substance caliber-of both salt and sweet
And yes-it recognizes to what I shape into bad and good
Add up these components-see it only as a scrupulous treat
Yet although you should establish a tie
Not fashions of statement-
No fixations or fabrications of fibbing-no lie
How to establish a bond and attachment between all of it
Sometimes I get burned out-unpleasantly
I only now see the assessment of others word to just quit
No-not for me-mental description of allows for more
And I do not anxiously work to no-end-refraction of that plus a mental bend
For this is not an infinite chore
Spoke in earnest to a physic-just the other day
Extraordinary-nonphysical-mental process
Of telepathy or future prediction
Which for some is bliss-a state of nearly a reasonable fathomable recess
Nothing of is which at all cause a restriction
Yet to speak-off the cuff
What exactly effects the mind or mental processes
In which chemical need-not be-maybe allowing euphoria
All senses alike-at a utopia type way of feeling
Get to that place of places quickly
Endure all that craving-watch all the healing
Hearing-sight-smell-
Touch-Taste
Covering all these bases plus more
And leave nothing behind in crazy circumstance-defined as haste
Chronologically-an order to the senses
Doing my wages-of the stages-despite all of these pages
My arsenal of artillery is far beyond-my consensus
Most in the aspect of yes-unnecessary baggage left for waste
I observe the charred remains-
And also notice the initial movement of my fork-depleted with rancid taste
Is it possible to see in which
Which is which which
And concluding with and proceeding from there
Are you a caress chin or a….Christian
A way to win
Learn abruptly from any type of loss
God is your maker-which signifies to a degree
That to an extent-You are your own boss

WRITTEN BY: Brian Moilanen

Congratulations

Possibly
Not the most well thought out or dubious award
Yet it has its understandable harmony utilizing agreement
In lay-mans terms-known as an accord
An accession this day-a common thank-you becomes rare
Call it growing together as a team with random kindness
It becomes a celebrated virtue that is both uncommon and considered a dare
Picked apart
An accomplice with undermining fate
Destiny this time-is it deranged or accomplished in succession
Get over the hump
A compliment is able to disregard depression
Learn the true access of the word titled irate
Anger fortified with sentiments of rage
Innocent I know I am
Yet still feel I am invoiced by unspoken letter to be in a cage
Minimum wage
Maximum work
Is there enough strident energy to turn my diary' page
Or opposing it-a distant smiling lurking shadow
One to fulfill my monotony's with congratulated splendor
Neglect I pray will not rear its ugly head
And send me unfairly on a weekend bender
Beneficence
A nice kind deed in which to promote
Compliment or a job well done
Of words not spoken-pride swallowed by a wispy throat
I know I am not a king
Because they do call shots and rules
Powers unique-the angel on high although does sing
And allows nobody to appear as unimportant fools
Adhere to what you will
And come of it what it may
Molded by not only the self
For at times the workplace feels as if molded clay
Praise
Thanks
Common word of great value
Re-invent Fort Knox
And the worlds will sell you
Agendas
Goals
Stamina from the long-winded
Helps the poor in wealth secure strength for the long haul
I heard from my neighboring friends
You bought yourself employment at the mall
Good luck
A statement worth its weight in gold
Prosper and live long
A cherishing glitz of grammar to keep you young- even if old

WRITTEN BY: BRIAN MOILANEN 2010

Connect the Dots

Habitually drawn in-or mysteriously drawn out
A connect the dots scenario of circumstance
Tints and shades of this here pen-they explain what humbling is all about
Or more to it than that
The fairness of connecting lines is firm with vitality
And equidistant they appear as pure black genuine yet flat
Connect those dots
Human mechanical beings
Search for a rising generation
And the working class blues-something real
Salient and with regard to showroom quality prolific
Possibly a merit of penetration with a way to heal
This paper is white
Accordingly this writer's creation is also colored with the color black
A game I am in is sufficient with members-plenty affixed
These lines form and seem to be connecting
And maybe a win of establishment equals to that of a crucifix
Or infinite answer to problems of inadequacy
They always contradict and unfold
And adhere such as frost to cold weathers glass
Maybe this parable of a sort-has already been told
If you're a rebel or rogue
Does this make any sense
Someone out there who designed this-and broke the mold
And relays back the last dot and always repents
So therefore do not listen to a pushy commanding
Effect or evil enemy
They or it can try
But with my gathered fortitude-will never command me
I am an aesthete
One in which who gives exemplified or exaggerated
Value to the artistic religious power of a cult
Because religion, politics, and government
Are maybe not directly spoken yet always a result
My joining of these black lines
From something within talking to the Roman Catholic Church
A string of black and white beads
Tinted and with jade-even every bead represents a sincere prayer
Pray one-pray for us all
To hush the cocktail hour naysayer
Or to the extinct unbelieving dinosaur crowd
With word be cautious yet vocal
For they with their view-can be barbarous and loud
My female companion also plays connect the dots
Of her assembly protocol at hand
Heck-if I could play the drums as her
I would also join that local hard rocking Christian band
As mentioned-this game of simplicity that I play
Call it connect the dots
Tedious work
Do not miss any spots
Visualize positive plots
Water the sweet smelling roses-inside the plastic pots
WRITTEN BY: BRIAN MOILANEN 2010

Cunning Game of Chess

Forget too soon
What you patiently gambled on
I am moving with my king
And courageously enough you make war against my pawn
A game supplied with hours endless
We might compete until the early dawn
Choose your battles wisely
And if need arise your demise
I could very easily revise
Equipped with quick wit and tenacious ability
A strafe possibly meeting its challenge and stalemate
I do see
And with this next move-intend to wait
Destiny or dereliction
Now be true-Which encloses upon your very fate
You claim neither
And freedom of chance engages into choice
Do not pick-and let destiny of path guard while guiding the way
An inner lesson learned-how although soon should we rejoice
The inner voice
Sometimes even a monkey on my back
I am swiping your game pieces
And readily do position them on a library of rack
Who will win
For I do not intend to lose
The fire is lit
And it is steadily creeping toward the fuse
Good luck
Both to me and the dogged you
Look within yourself for a hero
Now that is who wins
With this philosophy that is who fabricates as the few

WRITTEN BY: Brian Moilanen 2013

Deciphering Desires

A detailed person with intricate word
Not although as of the worldly-succumbed into money and desire
How to stay sane and within the Godly-does this sound absurd
Chilling is this sentiment that fuels the cold and strays from forever of fire
While engaged with enlightening soul and thought
Visions of both hate and love
A battle won-yet without physical confrontation was fought
Yet still a victory it is
A sanctimonious God is he who is sought
Found
Yes-found indeed
Harboring with assembly and holding pen and paper in hand
As I write blatantly I also do read
Feed this overcoming articulate passion-I will patiently stand
A unity of souls
Upon this tablet I currently do ink
Much more to add-do not hesitate or even blink
Keep your boat afloat with fidelity
And as for your character of soul-you will never sink
Do not allow for past despairs to unpleasantly haunt
Because if you allocate to this reservation
It will heckle your brave brain and also taunt
All pangs of mind games-also being singled out
Sight with and through our Savior's divine advent or plan
Not measuring egos-humbled despite obtaining clout
Deciphering desires
Furled with frigid ice and what is cool
Eliminates stress along with angry fire
Not allowing for lack of composure-not a fool
Be forthright while clinging to serenity
Even those deemed as medically blind will see the cure
In touch with miracles
That much I see and am quite sure
Rules that blossom
Whether playing for keeps
Or somewhat aloof and badgering that of an opossum

WRITTEN BY: Brian Moilanen 2013

Deja-Vu....or What

Technically
I suppose I should call this inadequate feeling a delude
Physically attacking- even an idol would add
Yet basically its demur is throughout my entire mind
As you know is this of genuine-and corresponded as glad
Deja-vu returns in rewind and once again you will find
That you are substantially either in backward or behind
Being tricked or even better yet
Finding your whole self in compliance with odd and absurd dido
Tricks
Games played on or about this human mind
Deja-vu alliance
Seems currently to be more of a...
Stubborn reborn brain mental reliance
You can't count on being or seeing supposedly- a situation more than once
Yet if calculated in the schools and hard knocks of this world
Is this supply more of needs than the profusion of wants
What does it matter
Becoming hallow-obscurely mentally inside
Fight or flight
I find the jet and co-pilot to manage this ride
What to choose for proper manner of expression of word
Not being drunk or high
Yet at the current moment my speech is slurred
Rambling I feel inclined to inform others of this observational fact
Line up those bowling pins
And a strike I will entail after what was racked
Yet indeed I do recognize this bowling alley
And if I had been here before I am sure I left behind a finale
I explain to the cultured and rude bartender my situation at hand
Yet walk away fitful as he calls me a cursed liar
I have been here before despite the temporary negatives in which they implore
I drink one pitcher of beer before analyzing the exit door
Chase me out of town
While chastising me in odd suit accompanied with orange wig
You have made me the buffoon; the local clown
Down to a few dollars
Nothing of commerce to bid or trade
If this were heavens Limbo
There would be slim chance any of them would make the grade
Armed with fortitude and my apparent strange ways
All the waitresses comment with is....
"Heys"
Or...."What do you need"
As if I were a problem without an answer to solve
Heck....The planets are definitely off course; maybe a sign of the end
Eventually the time will come and those spheres in the galaxy just won't revolve
As time has nothing at all more to lend
What a shame
From my parents I did grow, adapt and then so to say evolve
I have heard it said before-who cares-is he who wins
How although is this possible
For most of what I had was stolen for the record-downright even to my smile and its striking grins
Written by: Brian Moilanen

Demonstrations of Exploration

I speculate that I have been getting far beyond bored
Jump on the up going bandwagon
And continue to play a stimulating melodic chord
My mind has been made up for a while now
And an intertwined collage of promised word I do find
View the world
Seize the moment
Break free of the hypnotizing monopoly
And venture this land that was given and God sent
Count all my pennies
Add up my dimes
Next up is to decipher how many greenbacks that I actually have
For money is not a be all-end all
Yet....For this poor boys wounds-it's a protective and serious salve
Would someone care to join me
On this trip to somewhere subdued where warm palm trees are plunked
And in the heat of school yard basketball courts
Basketballs are plummeted and furiously slam dunked
Happiness is definitely not a true disease
Yet at the moment
I really do think I have an illness
And that illness has a name called joy
Maybe check out this town's stores
And buy a brand new adult toy
Or eat a hamburger-that is health minded and comprised up of soy
Maybe write a book
Which could supply the source of employ
I know-I will call up my past chum Roy
Who buy the way was an activist in the long eternal forever
Claiming if enough people were spiritually converted we would possibly say never
I finally round up my money and follow through with it all
Collapse of time has no chance in its form of contradiction
Which everybody knows
Is a leech like condition
And has the takers by way of infliction
It can drain physically yet environmentally it is flat out dramatic
My impression of....
Is consistent with what you think of me
Yet realize I will get a brand new chance
Picking with what I represent and where I stand
Travel
Journey
An orbit in which I would love to partake
Yet I confidently know I get unsettled
And it is altered such as a seismic earthquake
I could even travel with a bike with no air-the climb although would be firmly peddled
Vacation
Recreation time
Sweet as tea or soured such as a lime
I must pick my path
And dust off the sand and grime
I realize my existence has no exiting
And do enter into the forever and understand a gracious infinite time
Written by: Brian Moilanen

Digging for Gold

Am I getting old
We all know that nobody grows younger
I feel a seemingly relentless thirst
And taste a ravenous hunger
Digging for gold
At least enough to prosper some
Wise beyond talent
Will this remove what appears as glum
A human need-am I qualified to earn cash
As for daily bread-my plate is full of only crumb
I intently watched the stock market just yesterday
In hopes of shares skyrocketing
Just what to do and what to say
For I maybe ignorant
Yet miles away from being deaf or dumb
Some day stars and planets will dance in the sky
Call this if it applies as a boomer
Some day my personal relations will greatly increase
Or Is this just a self proclaimed rumor
Turning the page of my newest diary
I suspect to locate delight and sense the humor
No life so short that things can't turn around
This now felt satisfaction puts me in a stupor
Am I lost and not yet found
Being true to myself
No longer I believe do I need to scold
Listen intently children
As this story book hour is yet to be told
Everybody has the reigns to their own book
This chapter despite is complete-another chapter does fold
Grasping a better and more secure future
Now that is the altitude all Americans do behold
The end of this parable is now
And as for perseverance it is now spiritually sold

WRITTEN BY: Brian Moilanen 2013

Do-Did-Done

Do, did, done
Get your participles correct along with their proper tense
Figures of speech that represent correct verb forms
Knowing this were you right-or deemed impartial and targeted as dense
Is that the sky you see-beneath your wings
Or is it a zephyr of a steel barred vacuum that has you trapped
And the war-bird of hostility gestures as she conspicuously sings
Is it a done deal-has it all been tightly wrapped
A test
Or what….how should I know
This ferryboat of luxury slowly treads along the river
Although not capsized-I am tired and dragged endlessly with the undertow
I have been done
Because I just did
Will I become now with the sea life
And soon fraternize with the squid
Please alter what I attempt not to do
Am I right
Are you wrong
Formulas and maddening applications must now apply
Tell me-should I today wear a charismatic smile
Or watch what appears as a downside apparent- mutinous frown
I speculate besides all this
I am not the buffoon or beit the talk of the town
For I am far too educated and beyond that much too ….kind
Yet interesting as it may seem- melancholy finds my yesteryear
The good that I have partook in and had….could I please put it back into rewind
Sometimes my zebra coat keeps me completely and utterly warm
Yet other times it is frigid amongst all of the changes
And I do really feel as if even my closest of friends- could swarm
Yet why would they want to harm this Godly prophet
My profit sometimes is only in innuendo
And I wonder if the director of this film of life is up to his tricks
And cannot fix me because he has no needle with thread-no way to sew
Who determines and asks the revolving question
That I should say even if I not know what the answer is-hmm….what….don't know
Sequences and actions of series
My power and intellect of mathematics is fair
Yet I ask-what is the angle
And just what beside sheepishness….rests the dare
Or does the dare
Seem to grow wings- this servant asks his God
It fly's haphazard-despite having past records that appear to care
Am I sane or off just by a twist
Needing opened closets
They seem the only answer-Bi-God, yet also a way to resist
When does tomorrow technically end
For that matter when does today ever start
Have a solution
Because with it-comes the simplicity of an unbiased heart
I hope I equal to requirement of this occasion
Keep betting on the game and therefore rolling the dice
And please the Almighty first-somehow your life will find symmetry and get it done
WRITTEN BY: Brian Moilanen

26

Does Your Purity Exist

Occasionally wandering although aimless
Substantiated yet full attempts to still are completely blameless
Humbling achievements of the past have guided and claimed
Therefore such as and resonated as nearly shameless
Compassion fills my heart that is worn on my sleeve
Yet my mind wallows in my somewhat past muddied grief
Caused by disappointments that I rehearse and nearly believe
Purity is very difficult to find
And even harder to firmly hold
I am dressed for vibrant summer heat
Yet currently standing in the breezy rain and beside the chilling cold
By most I am considered quite angelically good
The deliverance of a saint's caress
Yet the meandering mind compensates with mental innuendo
And curiously engages to somehow undress
Soul with sight-sight with soul
Fabrication bounces the swinging yo-yo
And magically the child's hand begins to with insight roll
Have you ever noticed the serene purity
Of an infants or new babies tranquility of ways
Controlled by subjective environment
Sometimes these properties coalesce
Even when canonize into age old retirement
Genuinely good
Is this guiding-spirit
Addressed and understood
Conventionalized wisdom or the image of an angel
The noose around those devils necks
Yet forgive- and do not allowing for a horrifying strangle
Prayers being said
Beit the morning, lunch, dinner or late
All be sure-prayers of worth are heard
And through times etchings upon all grave stone slates
Flawless-yet refined with antique like sketch
Do you hear what I say
And see the logistics of my old school catch
Why spend every waking minute upon obtaining heaven
Live in the today
Keep much focus on the tomorrow
Unveil troubled days
To relinquish the past; and the sorrow
Yet credentials alone are…..supreme substitution
Purity
Keep clean in all ways
Obscurity
Dim light; thick haze
Security
Protection of self and soul and others to
Crudity
Practice when what is practiced practices you
How many times should we forget
Or are you torn in two-being uncomfortably split

WRITTEN BY: Brian Moilanen 2013

Don't Throw in the Towel

This name of mine has been dragged thru the mud
Calumny; character assassination and the absurd alike
How can I pedal a tipsy unbalanced unicycle
When my talents of action truly only allow for a bike
Cheap shots taken at me call for expensive retaliation
People apparently corner me from everywhere; beleaguered
Is it me versus the nation
Grab your artillery clips
Load the gun
Innocence forsaken
Because of thus so-it is now me on the run
And down I will not be taken
I have been hit with my fair share of shots
My varicose veins ruptured
And I observe of what should be healing clots
I am attributed by truth of word
Is there action attached to consequence
If so-have I been ousted or have I been simply ordained
I remember my past sorrows
And what reveals as everyday pangs
Hear me
See my body with action in cadence with its reaction
Triggered by your sick heart of malice
If I were king
How long would these problems remain at my chromium palace
Yet with time
Would I complete my purpose in concord with rhyme
Leave me alone
Yet in reference see me as a man who is usually alone
If you so wish
Call me on the silence of this telephone
Stick to your guns
Make sure not to turn off
All of your favorite liberated television re-runs
Silence yourself if you must
Yet in duplicity
Use your voice as a form of tolerance and trust
Depression may rear its ugly vile head
Yet be thankful for everyday of abundant health and life
Heck….a kind gesture with smile
Is what should find you when with or without your loving and deserving wife
Do not throw in the towel
People although display their pain to others
Love turns the tables
The formation of sisters and brothers
A battle is sometimes what it may seem
Yet if you adhere to the hope of integrity
God's love will eventually let you seize your dream

WRITTEN BY: BRIAN MOILANEN 2010

Dream If You Will

Generously spirited while beside myself I currently now do want
Gracefully I nudge myself and decide to vainly take
Capture
Take
Grab
Seize in what I speculate and what is deservedly owed
Outdoors the iced earth brings a plentiful blitz of precipitation
And the roads are glazed with outdoors ceilings that are snowed
The weather as mentioned is risky and the rounded clouds glimmer dark gray
Yet the vibrant sun envelopes me with its illusive distant warmth
Memorable days such as this were tabulated for good and to be cherished
Do some earnest soul searching
As obscure strange days of the past should just maybe be mentally perished
Forgive and forget
A Christian cliche-Or folklore that shouts for more
Am I good enough
Did I pass the test of your eternal rapport
A day of joy-would it not be great if euphorically it always did last
An age old adage
Yet not always heard from the past
Affection sustains while lack of positive change is chemistry of the mundane
What in your life(onward existence)-Is completely just superficial
Dot your I's
And please don't forget to initial
An adulated ego pleads to be even beyond authentic and genuine
A thought of enticement entertains my mind
How about a glass of fermented red wine
My full charged cell phone pleads for its telepathic use
I call up a past love
With conversation of unique and open voice
The talk being short in length yet not at full arousal
Splendor matching contentment
Now those similarities both definitely respond
I gaze as the conversation has just ended
As far off the pond in the yard is pristine enough just and shimmers
Ask yourself this imploring question
Wholeheartedly….What do I want the most
Possibly a worthy relationship with Almighty God
Being cushioned with sociable and showy rules with accordance to humble
A simple smile
An embracing hug
Principles that equate to necessities of everyday need
Customs that feel even greater than a recreational purging drug
Smell the roses
Thank-God for all and whom you have
Even the basics of a cup of hot black coffee
Although an adult-this statement may appear childish
Enjoy the sweet tangy mouthful of sticky tangy toffee
Our time on this earth is unusually short
In everyday possible-secure time to prosper and yet time for leisure
Pay your tithes to an abundantly gracious God
When the hours are growing long and weary
Allow time for rest-And take a nod
Love and be loved

For this is an almighty rule of customary format
Attentive to not allowing rule of being a door mat
Do not squander- make mental effort not to fail
Come as you are-being strong and not as sprat
Dream-As you must
Whether at sleep or while downright wide awake
For if possible ….It is an apex of absolution
And therefore concedes to its own formidable rules
Please live as free-going warriors without substitution
Strange as this may sound or apparently represent
Lives battle and battles are ongoing
Being forthright-include yourself as love-as loved ones when you repent
You will welcome your tomorrows with a smile
And now there is not as much too resent
Walk a mile-contemplate another mile-then get deserved rest for a while

Drop the Bomb (or not)

Beware
Modify immediately-and with caution broadcast what is partook
I may just drop a bomb
With you and yours being shattered-devastated and shook
Trust
Ha -ha
You denied-As I am only now unsound and recumbent of remaining to enslave
Me or you-you or me
Freewill versus destiny-which one will encounter the early grave
Prayers to God Almighty of wisdom sacrificing choice
Allowing an intermission rally in which happiness may just cling
Equivalent to its ratio leaves only to rejoice
Yet when do I draw the line
Sabotaged and destructed I need analysis of this opposition
This one manned army I highly believe-that you cannot defeat
Twiddle your thumbs in anticipation-a singular of any suspicion
A heart with no shackles
Compassion I will reply with
When I am at church
My minimum-I always at a maximum give-and pay a weekly tithe
Load your heaved guns
Ready up those tanks of fury
Abide by my totalizing plans
And for your sake quickly abort-get out of my way in a hurry
Out of what-out of my merciful choice of way
I am now subordinating as a reactor of defect
With only whispers to be heard-nothing at all truly audible to say
Happiness of yesteryear shall we not re-earn-noteworthy and to expectedly reflect
Is the countdown set or not
For on this plan of calculated warfare
You shall definitely see that an "x" marks the spot
Drop the bomb
Or get the kindling of devastation-burning and bombing right here
Calculations of war are doggedly everywhere
As the end of this badgering is almost done-have no fear
Yet this will only open amidst to chapter number #2
Which-as I think-allows for trouble and distress-and what next militantly to do
Should I have our forward observers sit back and patiently just wait
And find out if the rest of destiny can be more kind
The subsistence of derivative and confusing fate
War
Peace
Hostility harnessed nearly against itself
Increments of adjusted pain
Counting still although- only upon myself
I finally decide as an act of intimidation-to shed no more bombs
No more articulate mayhem
As I just got done speaking with my commanding officer
Her advice of ongoing peace-and only peace-I now give praise to General Kim

WRITTEN BY: BRIAN MOILANEN 2010

Exaggerations of Sadness

Externalized power
Assumption of gain
Specifically-although not material
Without cruelty it should grow and despite madness watch its gain
My world used to be quite simple
Yet your carved out passage is other than plain
Irony holds your glowing incessant lantern
And your mirror envisions only you-this is a stimulant to what is vein
Contentment that begins as conventional
Allocates to anybody and therefore the societal norm
And with your useful glancing stare is quite intentional
One-dimensional
You could become more if you weren't that shattered mirror
Within that mirrored glass I do stare
Fabrications and explorations of my mind proving I care for you
Are my days in steadfast sameness
Or can I rebirth them-can I renew
Mirror yourself –If you have the know-how and understand the explanation behind
What to exactly look for
Beyond that in stringent degree-what to find
I will fabricate and twist things in remedy in my favors so you may
The ice cream cone I graciously eat has its creamy zest
And almost reinforced it demonstrates its quality flavor
Tricked
Conflicting I am within every reason and rhyme
Take time for myself
All alone besieged by problems-I feel as if I have committed a crime
Anxiety disorder
Feelings of grandeur
Schizophrenia
How much am I able to fashionably endure
Maybe I suffer from humanitarian terms only
Stress
Overly proud in more ways than one
Spouting out words when I am aware of what I am doing
Examine yourself and the realms of your sorrow
The more you speak-is it only yourself that you are screwing
Tragedy
How many of these before you explode
Like a time bomb
Soon-without help and guidance-you could catastrophically explode
Reality separates itself both from dream alike and within a twisted fantasy
A conclusion
If you cannot separate these two worlds
You don't need major help-or even an institution
Yet do not deny
Sometimes a label can bring you down
Yet do not view a tragedy as an ongoing mess
Overcoming specifications and tribulations-stop the sorrows that are part real
Turn the negatives into positives-And God will conjure his workings and eventually bless

WRITTEN BY: BRIAN MOILANEN 2010

<u>Existent Time Always Is</u>

Existent
Time
Life
Death opens to life again
Add it all up
Yet...do not diverge so easily into sin
What about T I M E
It in itself is always somewhere
There
Here
Omnipotent
Opportune
At moments not....
Do not volunteer into it too soon
Not trying to scare you away
Life is so precious
And all that amounts successfully within its name
Life -some call it a game
Death-magnifies all with time
And brings strange willed fame
Rest in peace
Let the heavens bring more than glory
I will pay tribute and remembrance to your grave
To conclude your lives story
I love you
Always I have and will look you up in heaven
Graced go the numbers
Do not forget to tally the spiritual number-which is 7
The earthly complete number is 4
Yet you need much more than that
To enter the pearly gates heavenly door
A reminder although-that time or existence
Does not ever-ever end
While on earth being a sinner we all are
Faith dominates religion
More than religion dominates clergy
Almighty God
The power is far too far from what we can understand
Communion
An earthly union
That lasts down to the last sip of holy wine
Of heavenly institution with
Sacrament that fills the body as totally fine
Some say time ends with the last breath
Religious intervention begins with....
A soul
Belief
Suffering and grief
Inspiration from a guardian angel
Guidance more than the self can possibly bring
Now lets talk about true life
No more pain
No more strain
No more theft

Only battle left is to win over a soul to God's never-ending garden
Where you can honestly say…
God is my freedom warden
Get ready for round 2 of a life without heat
Only cool sunshine with light breeze
Now….Is that not cool
Guardian-angel-saint –archangel-pope of prosperity in peace
Be honest
Is this not the ultimate never-ending release
Forever
Untimely
Infinite
Never missing a beat
Ossification
All leads to a permanent resuscitation

WRITTEN BY: BRIAN MOILANEN

Extremely Subtle

Fine-drawn
Persuasion
It is subtle enough
To fit the memoirs record of occasion
Delicately crafted-nearly and almost insidious
That is cooperative if you respond utmost congenially
And play a bluff as nearly oblivious
Is this too small for impacts installment
For lives practice and procedure
Hush-hush
Lives recourse is complacent on what we must endure
Yet sanctification requires as a medium I guess
Of what is absolute-and what should remain as pure
I recall completely and entirely
The so to say anonymous display from participants-being with her
The past experiences relate to well being
Have a quieted faith prominently including strategy
Hmm...Is this what the future holds for seeing
Secretive so to say
Flattery of silence to the socially skilled
I am a man of God
Therefore with reason this Creator has pleasantly had me willed
To conquer
To prosper
To succeed while not allowing to oppress
For I won accept but I can't neglect
A friend or partner that is she
Until death do us part-with or without quandary protect
You the public eye
Might be my biggest enemy-saturated with wine- I do suspect
I feel myself falling into that downward vertigo spiral
Or should I in religious terms-call it the abyss
I will resurrect
I will and shall gain the eternal respect
A white lie may turn into a black realm of indecisive hatred
Be careful where you step
You know-Be cautious upon where and what you do tread
See the colors of full- spectrum
And not only red
A little secret
A hint of what humans do
Now you hold the saving ratchet
And is it me that does screw
Keep the faith
Do not lie or deceive
For in the end –Beit years gone past
Not much does that method relieve
Hush-hush
Good day
Let your emotions lead
And not show-just prove the proper way

WRITTEN BY: Brian Moilanen 2013

35

Feeling Your Pain

Disheartening
Maddening
Sadness dilutes itself without liquid through the heart
A one -time life of happiness
Suddenly-smack dab falls disproportionately apart
I do not know the source of the pain that you are convinced you feel
Can I be a catalyst for chemical neurological modification
Or does this situation seem to be almost more than real
I feel your pain
I sense what you are going through
Because what is going thru is exactly what you sense
Do not refrain or say much more
I am not dense- as these storm clouds will
Soon hopefully be gone-A promise from a prophet who is sure
Everybody somewhere
Figure of speech and matter of truth-has it worse
Change can come at an instant
Therefore do not let pain reckon or rehearse
Yet I am not blind to what you are going amongst
Going through
Problems steady now in your life
Yet all of us sometimes unfairly
Gamble with disharmonious strife
Beit mental-emotional-physical-or even psychological
Creates anguish and throws life all around-off balance
Amazing the byproduct of these arbitration's of discomfort
Could you say this oddity has its own talents
I will pray
I will yet be pragmatic
Realistic of and how to treat a battered soul
At heavens gate-yet not now
I will continually pay the redeeming toll
Consult me if you need a judge in your case
Bad health-wasted years
Are determinant upon how you play the cards
If you falter and need emotional hope
Is there a need to mention the hospitality of mental wards
Maybe find a pope that could put you in the magnification scope
We are all included in God's plan
Check the stats of biblical truth
In this race of spirituality we all have ran
If you have not run for grace pursuing God
Wake up-feet trace amongst the
Planted weeds and green sod
Searching for the land
The promised land
Will that serve as a passage to pacify your pain
God loves you no matter what
God loves you
Even if with only the self you have fought
Do not surrender
This battle with pain you shall inherently win
Throw away that frown
And freely obtain this gift-call it an eternal grin
WRITTEN BY:BRIAN MOILANEN 2010

Forbearing on a New Agen

Knowledge
Superhuman IQ
Intelligence
Competing with robots
Computers make their stand
Human methods falter
Yet they are in serious need and still in command
Formalized with civilization
90's IQ range quotients just for tots
Living in this advanced age we most certainly do
Now days the haughty and only inwardly lead
Tread more on themselves and often in hurried haste
Their planned escape-Do run from baited cheese and also from dread
Geniuses
Some are far to witty to understand
Human intervention
Simplicity of good versus bad intention
Theatrics sometimes bluntly dumbfound ones with that impede
Social and clique gathering order and direct
For lives pages of choice or plot to commonly read
Gatherings of the college masses
While strangely inquietude keeps others antisocial inclined to their dorms
Abstaining from this situation
Or any at all for that matter
Is that of abstaining at a library on wheels station
Climbing downwards recession is coward-which way on a two way ladder
For the record
Which way does it spin
And for that matter-at what speed
Will these anti-socialism spin doctors abruptly play their part
For making it correctly justified in this world someone needs a heart
If incognito-put your supplies of machinery in a shopping cart
Computers
Cell phone
Plans not working out-quiet rage
Am I writing too fast-continue back to the start and reread the page
Back to where I started
Anchoring to the middle age
Should I promise everyone even with miniscule detail
If so-I will be back rock hard and keep my valiant pledge
A new age
A new millennium
Science and technology so headstrong and virtually without risk
Am I right
Or shunned silently by the elderly...tisk .kh...tisk....tisk
Who knows it all
All of it knows who
Linkage of marriage takes the opposites
Joining them up as one-although there is two
Welcome someday to a night living in
A vacuum enclosed world inside the hemisphere contained directly inside the moon
True-I maybe slightly crazy
Yet not out of sight and out of mind
Therefore-crazy as the loon
By the way
I was born precisely at noon
Speaking intercessional-and always as an expressional
I hope my extraverted-ness has not spoke too soon

WRITTEN BY: BRIAN MOILANEN-2010

Generally Speaking

Generally speaking
Usually not as the darkest of souls
I reckon that truth chooses sides
As everything else pays retribution-yes it also extols
Sweet yet accompanied with what is bitter
Forgiving and forgetting fuels me as full
Most people would agree that I am not a quitter
Yet strangely a side of me
Involuntarily still adds up on yesteryears resentments and regrets
An angry path of reprisal sees a less followed path
Comprised of sporadic bullets with bloodshed
Angry retaliation also has its wrath
Now don't you wish that you were dead
Gasping your last breaths
And found as deceased and laying on your bed
Misfortunes
Unanswered prayers
I have often times been deceived with trick
With a conglomeration of uneducated naysayers
Malice or merely unjust black magic-I am he who is sick
Dear God-I intend to fail you not
Scrutinized onward Christian soldiers
An untimely battle occasionally is lost
Consecrations
Serve your Almighty God
Preach to be heard by all nations
Throw out the big bang theory
Because a life without Christ and Jehovah God
Is understood by some yet is even more than scary
Become better or bitter
Or locate a middle ground indeed
Cultivate your progress and see the soul
The instruction book you make as you also do read

WRITTEN BY: Brian Moilanen 2013

God - The Ancient Entity

To my sincere loving Creator
Within mankind's understandings-you are the God with existence in reality
And yes-also within our minds
Ultimately placed and twisted together-all that surrounds
Confidence insisted-I will say that you entreat what is chivalrously entreated-what is entwined
The crowd of religion has claims it has all been enshrined
Must I add that the Almighty has constructed
Put it together
Perfected
Reverence paid for us-as if being resurrected
Connected
All people form an allegiance that seems if so sternly suggested
A freeing of that mental prison or warfare that we are in
Breaking of those shackles-and not any longer being arrested
Accusers perplex and utterly annoy
The prejudiced meticulousness haphazard some have protested
Not words that are profound
Yet keep in mind that heaven-compared to earth
Has much more to offer-and is phonically sound
One truth
That should be all humans sincerity-believers and nonbelievers
Do I need to take a wage-a poll
An unbiased poll-only based upon obeying understood as clarity
Clearness of our all powerful God and his righteous following son
For that matter-Through all 66 books of the Holy bible
Salvation was significantly raised-and yes-salvation was won
God as you know
Existed prior to the being of whatsoever- anything else
Before even the powers of dark and light
You must gather intrigue for this ongoing situation
And not ever be afraid of the holy word-or even the instance of fight
Contrivance
Only a God of this power could lovingly produce or give so much
Call these people-believers
Who are continually guided and doing so forthright acquire the special touch
Read the book Genesis to get an understanding of our God and eternity
Then after those other important biblical books
Read Revelations-choose your side-Bi-god and he will answer the justified plea
Collusion
Through astonishment alone
End the mind confusion
Introduce
More people to God for heavens sake
Produce
The life worth living keeps the word
Reduce
Complications and all problems abroad
Induce
Pass on the magic without the needle
Soon-yet far way from today
Heaven and eternity employ the robust
And within this angel of light
Beit by my past track record-you can confidently trust
WRITTEN BY: BRIAN MOILANEN 2010

When I Will Be Gone Forever

Indescribable
Contents that are such as this
Are long and winding down-nearly insurmountable
Do not confute
Just reimburse and commute
Please-no arguments at this given time
What comes around goes around-only within me you might dispute
Privileges-awards given upon benefit granted and to be enjoyed
You concluded I was not worthy-somehow deemed wrong I became
Which what comes from the inward psyche-the numbers tally-I am annoyed
When I am gone
I will be gone forever
All of this wasted time-I am welcomed to the never
Yet my actions will be continued
Do not mind it being a new home-a new town-a new place
I anxiously await to be definitely absorbent renewed
Stuck in a situation that comforts more
I would define this as being….glued
I need a taste of spice and speckle of salt
Going day to day seemingly aimlessly
I will be gone soon-you can add me up as gone-the final result
Others say I need to surrender-to your love
Yet there is none-none at all
Two-living under the same roof
I feel as if crumbling-and intimately aloof
With my life
People suggest
Into situations I need not want to be
They subject
Because you cannot pull a living man from the dead
In which with me-you cannot promote to resurrect
Analyze my life
And let me….yes me suggest
Ghost town blues
I would not worry-all that pseudo falseness
Nobody-is advanced enough to give even a truce
Where should I go
I am now estimating-yet not geographically in tune
It is April now
Yet my escape is not on schedule until June
I promise that….
I will disappear
Gone before your eyes even blink twice
We do not see eye to eye
Do you-or I-not fully understand
I am a visionary who is correct
And will follow Christ further-and am in command
We do not read from the same book
Or the same page-In silence
I will attempt and concede at fulfilling my silent inner rage

WRITTEN BY: BRIAN MOILANEN 2010

<u>Guilty of Innocence</u>

Unwillingly- almost plagued by this nearing restriction
Cross your T's-dot your I's
And avoid in all terms a glaciating time warp contradiction
Games that people play often times are not revoking – filled with malice
Slanderers
Character defamation
Lies
It took coaxed angels to write and concede with the Declaration....
Of Independence-that is moreover to mention
The winning bid that was declared and created
To establish freedom infinite for those.....
1776
Was this the year to be forever known and taught
Both to humans and the advent of all cultures-including all form
Add to your own studies exactly what should just be sought
And maybe the innocence of-shall find a societal depository norm
Devils versus angels
Or is it the other way around
If you ever uncover that buried dead innocence
When and where Christ will also be collaboratively found
Yet innocence dies
And guilt by the assailed-now is all that exists
And freedom of freedom-now only is harnessed while truth only denies
Guilty until proven innocent
Is that the disguised truth in justice
A social disease-neurosis with attached psychosis
Humanitarianism
Off by a few marks
Cut through this deep and thick hog wash
And embellish if you wish-uttering with solemn remarks
Irony
Can you not hear the-non evidence
And see the branding iron of possibly a....number 4
Forgiven
Despite why some play so heard just too be dead
Doomsday
I do not think so
Keep God in your hand and he will keep
Your hand with faith- in the heavens
Holy sevens
Spiritual sevens
Good convenience stores out there
7-11's
May
Say
Some-Way
A life full of utter dismay
Not acting-not even with my psyche
Yet still observing your play
Guilty of Innocence
Can you keep up with you and me
Honestly
Keep up with yourself and within this crowd
Turn it up to sixty decibels-and not down
Because with me the volume is always respectable
Yet....
Muddled
Fiddled
Thrown in the pot-yet not griddle
WRITTEN BY: BRIAN MOILANEN 2010

Handful of Hearts

An angel's zeal possibly within my own hands
Silencing nagging and intolerant inner demons
Which in turn make persistent unforgiven commands
Ultimately owned by God I am
Books of holy prophecy-as I do study and fervently cram
Green fragrant smoke
Billows up and utmost high
Seven leaves of this marijuana
A deity that you just cannot deny
Yes now is a new time to modify lives cards
That is if need be
The rusted saint entertains Christianity
Take a bow and live a life that is rewarded and full
10 commandments-a method in which I rightfully do incline
Take a stand emulating with pull
A colossal creator being omnipotent and everlasting
Blindly you can see still see resurrection's holy sign
A handful of hearts
The engine churns as it also turns
And how to end-the beginning of all important starts
Even flow
To try and to be tried
Which way is up-my intentions of are just where to go
Escaping fantasy which makes way for a new reality
A gracious gift from our our giving Jehovah God
Escaping with absolution and not major calamity
A world beckoning with hope
And as for freedom it sustains and always does see
An ordained painting of you
Along with a significant snapshot picture of me
How can you not agree
My story of beating triumphant hearts
Is maybe my goal
Along with only just love
Has its price but ye never a fee
A short story of affection shining with angelic force
Repent and seek salvation
Oh...of course
Hmm...a new song with outstanding beautiful chorus

WRITTEN BY: BRIAN MOILANEN

Hard Act to Follow

Do you ever become awestruck with strange uncertainty and blindly follow
Is the life you lead with sufficient serenity
What is the exact substance that could help who is wispy and hallow
Observe the ordained or self promoted as great
Inherited merits of status
What others call exemplified resources to fervent fate
Earned
Watch the pendulum swing
How much of this prominence was actually pertained; and how much learned
How about yourself
In the way of judgment-do you have good rapport
For that matter-examine your own family tree
Please tell me-now just what encompasses your formalized folklore
Hard act to follow
Be honest-soul search yourself for an answer-say even by tomorrow
Will you surpass what precedes you
Or do you weaken and become the anti-benefit of someone else sorrow
If back in yesteryear would you become a simpleton-to entertain the palaces noble
Laugh at the silly antics of this paid one's entertainment
Or maybe paint pictures of demons in the mines of cobalt
Seriously
Where do you stand
Director of dissonance
Being out of harmony with sound and sometimes even reason
Or a General of good and forthright guidance
Who would never turn against and commit unruly treason
I have heard it said that one of the toughest commandments to follow
Is to not desire or covet your neighbor's goods
Yet isn't a hint of jealousy- by both parties
And surrounded by the vertigo-of the misunderstood
Not into giving in to doing wrong
But an attempt to let my miniscule or colossal voice be heard
For on this world I am just another number
And against the odds
Am hauled at a slow speed rate-such as lumber
Leave behind a good name
For in heaven it is worth more than gold
Another anonymous fable
That will not weather or ever grow old
For this is what my Father has said to me
Administering not discernment
Yet a grave in-scripted with goodness-also emotions of both tears and glee
It is valid
With my actions spent-the goodness spoke of me
Yet in truth-I am not dead yet
Despite the odds-place your virtue upon my open hand
And God
Yes God-Will find a way with victory to win this poor mans bet
Hard act to follow
Both for you and me
Internalized somewhere prior to your conception
And I do believe-God will see you thru
Salvation-Sureness of word
And everything in-between and even beyond
I pray-such as for me
This undying love for life-grows from beyond the title fond

WRITTEN BY: BRIAN MOILANEN

Her Immeasurable Soul

I search my wife's immeasurable soul
Waiting to prosper upward and ascertaining onward
I do pay the wage that is financially burdened-complicated is the toll
I concede my prayers ideally to the Holy Bible
Which presents itself as a beacon
Bearing light-an illumination in which to read
Such as a lone wolf-I do readily hunger
And obtain surely my daily feed
Letting go of an uncertain past
And secondarily steps to forgive
I stock up on needed essentials-and follow a newly typed cast
A goodness that lasts and a more righteous path it sets
Analyze her being-find where this reddened heart does lead
Flesh and blood
Versus salvation of sanctuary along with soul indeed
This pertains I suppose to just who is holy
I beg for forgiveness-as tears turn blood red and abundantly bleed
Avidly turning and listening to counsel
Interventions totaling as sufficient and being a planted seed
Deep sincere prayers only understood by an angel
Lead by the most pure in heart-for they obtain the highest seat
steps to take-venturing for a medium as a win
Beginning small and mildly abrupt
A path lesser taken-while abstaining from sin
Temptations you know are booming with volume and what is corrupt

WRITTEN BY: Brian Moilanen 2013

Hole in My Pocket

Have I ever specified what money and fiscal attributed pleasures mean
Call these resources- if you will...
Currency
Cash
Legal tender
Dough
Bucks
Or monetary necessity so I am able to see
See my dreams and also see my security
If you have too little
You play with cards dealt on a stacked deck-as you can obviously see
Or did you become one that spends it all
And only on your own poor judgments of circumstance
Did you become the postponed-take the leap and accept the fall
I suppose or understand that I have my baggage
Yet who has cast the first stone
For I know without a word spoken-that only my luck I have stroke
Despite my situation now-I am broke
Busted
Reduced to poverty and the like
When I play I go for it all
Give me a cigarette and off the match I will light
It is always like looking at a small 4 squared wall
No
Although innocent
My mode of thought is drawn upon the incessant characteristic of conquest and confused thought
For I obey except for the references of drink and smoke
My lungs become filled with vapor s of gray fog
As my brain channels and does not choke
Did you get a healthy toke
My first time was not with my parents-yet with everyday common folk
So ash out now-and instantly you will realize what it is to catch flight
Cook up a customary meal
And have a bite to eat
Back to my problem
Or is it my answer
For if you do not have enough
It is like living with a deadly malignant cancer
And when you have too much
Everyone emulates as a friend or pal
Characters of hypocrisy and friends provided by your fate
Realize now your selections
Do you feel as if a politician
And are canvassing your parties before your elections
Hole in the pocket
Pocket in the hole
Do you now perceive the connection
That money can end wars-even bolster an election
Say what you want
And I am sure that you will
Must I add that being without money
Is connectedness to a spacey, odd and all uninspiring thrill

WRITTEN BY: BRIAN MOILANEN

Hound Dogs of Howell

Turn your reluctant cheek
Become silenced by the meek-yet still changing as... hungry
Within only the brain now- does that distance of space speak
Honesty invades and the howl escalates
Maybe an attempt to not let in even the neutral
Yet off course-my mind rummages with circuses and parades
This noise accompanied with the passing exclusive scenery
I see a billboard with a picture resembling love-just like you
Yet undeniably I turn blue-as you claim it must be me
What I cannot erase or mildly fabricate even from thought or deed
I watch intently at those hound dogs-now do run
My eyes become mesmerized by their provocative canine speed
The pursuit
Engaged I watch the chase
Restless hound dogs of Howell
Always feed-and anxiously keep eye upon their pace
A division of man versus animal
Neither to an understanding that would easily direct
Or snatch the fishing pole and unnecessarily eject with pull
This almost ordained and lit-up city
Fashions itself with crime and violence of low
A zebra nations fashioned with both black and white
Observe the crowd of gatherers comfortably flow
Houses and homes of all style, shape, and size
Yet somehow they almost always seem to exist
So if not broken-is it time to revise
The hound dogs of Howell
Distant-yet spacious and therefore not completely alone
As you know-without a trace of prominence-things are able to get foul
Agriculture
Lined with bright sun and its yellowing shine
Blue soft skies of beauty
Are now equipped with a car ride that is dandy and fine
My mother and I pass a farm
As she says poignantly to my almost cathartic me
It is the simplicity of-this creates its almost vigorous charm
I spot a hound dog's unleashed vacant home running with his yard
All the roughed up grass within that plentiful resort
My eyes catch a glimpse of a tear
I allow the emotion that is both sway and preponderance
I gently sob yet not see any weights-any fear
We pass the house
The dog chases and howls in delight in Howell
A bark like noise yet not of fear
Yet attached with emotion-a relief to these bodies of whole
An acknowledgment of inner resources
Letting the serene of conscience know-that they have an eternal soul
My closed eyes this night find myself nearing sleep
Another year-or years of this is what I need
Without witness my soul does invade the greatness of this moment of day
For I am human
And my feeling not anything that of disarray

WRITTEN BY: BRIAN MOILANEN 2010

How Much Does it Take?

How much
How much does it take
Of viable sin and bondage before our gracious God does snap
Do you see the residual virtue to commence the wrath
Is joy itself infused-with hands that triumphantly clap
See the advent and invitation of before the invasion of endings
Earlier than the disclosing of revelations wrap
Lust
Murder
Envy
Jealousy
A few precursors before and prior to the final end
Wickedness
It lasts
Even with the supplements of a sinning war waged smile
Hang in there
Mankind's transgressions will only last a short more while
Who knows the exact date-this abolishment is pertained with planet earth
Keep in mind if modified with change it may not be too late
As Christ walks the earth again and incarnates his opportune chance at rebirth
Archangel Michael
Are you ready to wage war against Armageddon and Satan
Do the archeological doctrinations now
And learn to convert as you pertinently discipline
Pray
Not only for thyself and loved ones-yet enemy to
Voice yourself and bellow with the onward Christian soldiers
If your insomnia this night is lasting
You might be drinking too much Folgers
Eternal benefits
God vindicates his word with judgment and concern
As you know-believers of God or not-we all do learn
Jehovah's house is to be a house of prayer for all nations
Shall we call this a birthplace of creed, culture and vital religion
If you do not believe in an Almighty God
Is it possible that you may
This is your choice
And even choice sometimes and usually can be formed clay
There will come a time when every knee will bend to Jehovah
When the critical times of this land pervade
Is it true the very perils of this human race are not yet at ease
Can we as a whole escape the war to end all wars
Intervention of the holy word is corrupted
And is even less evident and available in your local book stores
Should we accept a broken faucet that continually and with divergence leaks
As told by the scriptures of Daniel the Messiah was cut off of and desolated
For the exact period of 69 painstaking weeks
Another example of end times
Complete the riddle
To settle intact the persuasion of rhymes
True we do not know exactly when
Yet with events such as Revelations scripture-do not seal up the words of the prophecy
Of this scroll, for the appointed time is near-may be factual with all sin based glory
That God will bring it on and hard
To complete Revelations and end this bible of loves story

WRITTEN BY: BRIAN MOILANEN 2010

Howell's Haunted House

A significantly old sullen home
Located somewhere between country and vast fields
Bestowed with ironic poltergeist intervention
Diabolically intervened tension is what this yields
Visits although from where-understood as the grim 5th dimension
Embodying an eerie age-old superstition
Where even the courageous-decipher amongst all this tension
Mysteriously following is an enveloped place of limbo
That some are purging and in a punishing plateau of purgatory
Where those who lived on the edge of sin-might understandably go
The vacant brown and gray home appears as broken
Not to mention tattered and torn
Sentiments of an ill logic chasten
As a defiance to the law of love resort to an apparitions scorn
Trails of dancing white lights
Sealed shut windows represent defiantly dancing curtains
And an attic door becomes carved with those who passed on years ago
And were said to be completely forever lost
However how to save these pillaged souls
Beyond that-will there be a fiscal and emotional agonizing cost
A chiseling view of the dispirited
The clock on the wall now just does not turn or tick
Time literally is standing still
My consciousness of deep soul becomes vile and ultimately sick
Even I am maybe am recognized as different
Now I intently view this trail of ghosts
A strange sense of communication-from them to me
As for my senses-they are separating and also aroused
A nearing stench of spoiled fragrance represents lucidity
An untimely sight again plays havoc to me
As a once off television quickly turns on and off
The lost soul trapped within the quivering channel
Is a deceased friend of old
Screaming at me to get away and leave him alone
Next occurrence is the ringing of a non existent telephone
A true spectacle
This paranormal is evident and real
And booming loud is the tone
Somehow I fall asleep as if in a trance
Poltergeist happenings in Howell are corrupt and of truth
I am now a firm believer in what is beyond
And perpetuated forward as even a super sleuth

WRITTEN BY: Brian Moilanen 2013

Human or Not

Organic, bionic and electronic
Draw back the syringe with needle implementing its serum
Will you discover the speed of sound; transpiring what seems as sonic
Am I a cyborg
Or that of something else in which I pertain
You know-A freight train could not do me in
You will witness me walk upright disdaining of troubling pain
CAT-scans
E.K.G.'s
E.M.G.'s
Still not yet withstanding being out of holy prayers reach
Witness the skeptics- as I am in prayer upon these hardened knees
Occasionally I have vivid daytime nightmares of things creeping out there
Hallucination or a dreamer's nightmare
In hopes of reaching my target or merely a dream scrape
I wish the vision were as a new Corvette within a explicitly arranged garage
Am I human
I do understand emotions with their attached feelings
I have survived a wild and poor dream yet while staying wide awake
Which I suppose helps me with my lives cards- hocus-pocus dealings
I honestly have observed U.F.O.'s
Even spoken to an angel within kind regard
And argued blue-faced with a genuine devil face to face
All within the realms of a psycho ward
You name it
I have been there to battle until competition did end
In retrospect
Did the games of life foolishly and with drainage begin
The more obstacles that surround me
Pours in the allowance- or is it remission of sin
Why won't these tribulations end immediately now-so I can become free
So I may become even more of a stronger man
Intrinsic uniqueness
Eccentric completeness
Take liberty and never lose sight-beit dreams or goals
I.Q. Scales that are individual
Yet always arrange themselves as residual
How much power does this supposed human brain hold
E.S.P.
Telepathy-what and without word has plainly told
E.M.I. scans
Equate into valuable medical plans
No longer a poverty stricken genius
Finding myself rummaging hungry in the midst of garbage cans
Go back to the beginning of my candid review
If I am part medically artificial
What constitutes brain and body to function-even that as new
If I am old then –is the latter half statement then not true
The mold of the radical preacher-and now just wondering what to do
I am yet intact but feel as the lonely-the few

WRITTEN BY: BRIAN MOILANEN 2010

Hypnotic Voltage

Impact induced hypnotics-a slowed hibernation type anthem sets in
Along with its extra strange electrical stimulation
The measure of a secured voltage-impeccable yet not in violation causing chagrin
Brain in method seems totally in manipulation-sort of smashed up
Torn in two-striving to locate myself as one
As I expected these parameters of regions gather intellectual power-do not shun
Yet as for their genius-what is there remaining to do-locate my inner self for some fun
Explorations of the hypnotic voltage
Transmitted
Appreciate the worth of what is transmuted
And altruistically what has been refuted
Expand the marvelous brain
Encourage the soul to work in unison with the mind
Days charge forward with unexplained periods of foisted depression
So in this experiment-what is it exactly that we look to find
Something or someone somehow to be gratefully appraised
If I appear lackluster
It is primarily because I am in the mix-a frenzied daze
No bluffs as if I were playing poker
No gamed allowed performing those tricks deemed inappropriate
Matter of fact is language of this test
Reprogram chemistry if need be and possible-I have just openly confessed
The workings of obsession
Eternal or supposed world like suppression
Those two do not work hand in hand
How can this muddied water be pliable
So much done to change myself and my thinking
Have I paid back emotional wrongs where it would be called reconcilable
Yet it began with apparently watered sand
I can now ultimately feel the powered voltage
Or is it dormant and held without sizable ransom
Place your bets-if gutsy raise the ante
Now focus on all that cash-does it not become handsome
Electricity
This point in time-powered at great length amongst the entire brain
Call it a colossal weathered brainstorm
That is nearly plagued with its acidic rain
I must add-I was randomly chosen for this medical procedure
Some call it a strange science based vow that I have captiously made
Yet will it mentally crush me-with my name dragged thru the mud
Or find me on the beaches-catching sun also while finding shade
Brain waves
E.S.P.
What about the 6th sense
By the way-do you agree
Life a journey gathering up a journey
Through space
Racing against time
Sanguine comfort
Sober-yet difficult in walking that thin line
My cranium becomes a star considered by the branch of science
To me it is valued nothing more than the kitchen sink
Or should I explain myself-I will call it a reminisced appliance
Good luck to you
And also good luck to me
Between the dawn's and dusk's here
This operation allows medical science to continually see

WRITTEN BY: BRIAN MOILANEN

50

Hypochondriacs and Other Stuff

Sickness
It pervades and invades seemingly when things are already at the worst
If you are a wailer when burdens mount
Have you readily rehearsed
Something is wrong
When perpetually something has went generally right
Are you putting on the weight a little too quickly
And are the newest pants that you own significantly getting too tight
Do not overreact
Keep yourself in check
For making a big deal to the obvious masses
Only is transformed as a big production
Symptoms like this heck- they need their reduction
If you should forwardly move forward in this worlds production
What about your muscles ability in unison with the brain
Can or cannot it be reduced
So that we are able for less melancholy-and open allotment for much more joy
For at subject at hand
You can't and won't put a quarter in me for five minutes of mimicking a toy
Strange brain
Rejected body
Blinding eyes
Is this a new-found shattering commodity
Is there a genetic basis too all of this
If so and yet if not
Could this presence of the medically lost ever find bliss
So much to learn
Inside myself even-compassion seeds must propagate and grow
For we all have our problems
It is within those deemed irregular and not with the most
That get there's
And often day- dream of life on the beaches and the southern coast
What about D.N.A.
Ribosome
Skeletal makeup and everything else in-between
Sometimes the simple man is more than content
As he ventures into the serene
Sometimes you may be sick
Often times it is even carved out that you are not
Remember that the x is the component
And that the defined location marks the spot
Health although is not a game or a puzzle to solve
Yet if this were the case
Where did the Cro-Magnons and even earlier Neanderthals evolve
And moreover-what in exactness did they solve

WRITTEN BY: BRIAN MOILANEN

I Could Wait My Life

Does this all weigh-in….or uniquely enough
Wait upon my peculiar thought with answering alike
I have readily observed the yesterdays
And my nearly surrendering brain-claims to possibly go on strike
A whole life of waiting-for the good life and its arbitrating with
This one piece of special gold I have-has its spectacular touch
And is taking its ride to the notable pawn shop-or beit blacksmith
It has its sentimental making that claims to….contain love within-very much
Charm and grace of what appears as divine
Yet in just a moment-someone else's hands of ownership-it will sadly go
Money for a weeks-supply of cash-not to mention-a night on the town where I can steadfastly dine
Assigned a meek hand that always although-supplies my soul
Possibly all predestined-a clean slate of tenacious hope
I throw the dice-as onward they do stroll yet cautiously continue to roll
I could wait my life
For castles in the sky and also out on a newly remolded pristine land
I watch the clock of virtue
And see if prayer stretches out the day-with plenty of further more going sand
I wish
I crave
I have a longing and a yearning
Which ignites an inner candle representing prosperity and peace
And I can apparently always see it burning
Serenity-a piece of my perspicacious mind
Is choreographed as a –peace of mind
The path you lead will not completely leave you alone or be
You will form friends of genuine
An embarked loyalty towards oneness…..you will always or soon see
Sure
I apply myself-yet often feel the slap on the face-of repulsive rejection
This someday will all forthcoming welcome-
A generous exception
On the flip side of this tails up coin
Awaits myself a second-possibly even a 3rd chance
That and this awaits my psyche
A generous mans rarity-a coded tonic-circumstantial romance
Straight laced
Or to become ever lifted highly with a drink
Yet do I truly desire that
In vertigo or is it passion-my emotions are on the brink
If I fathom what could be for too long
The past might spell or recreate another ending
Belief-reconstructs a broken heart and mind-and all that was once wrong

WRITTEN BY: Brian Moilanen 2013

Illustrated Conceptions

Tedious and long
Maybe even somewhat boring instilling lack of interest
Must I add-literally very drawn out
Is this voice talking to you or me
Disregard-For I have not the time to listen to you pout
Seen from nearly everywhere
Is it television from the skies with its illustrated conceptions
Or maybe cabin fever with its rattling deep abound
These stories that harness seem to find me
And henceforth tweak with a remote subtle sound
A minor soft hint
Or is it a screaming yell
Not reasonably quite sure of myself
As this planet borders between both heaven and hell
What your informing ears and eyes do see
The brain develops further onward
And signifies occasionally with- just leave me be
Is that plasma television watching you
Or by chance-is it the other way around
Deception of reception
More to be found
And therefore a lot more to be heard
Distant echoes from strangers
Now does that not seem currently absurd
Care, concern with caution put forth
I am receiving as well as giving
To this God with his angels-Straight from the North
Of all lives actions and reactions
Try never to over speculate or get too emotional
Do you feel the mantles core of earth shake and shift
And can you recognize the barbaric stronghold pull
What remains to a life that has
Recently just flown to the stars
Although keeping a low profile
Tinted windows represent your arsenal of cars
And while golfing utmost competitive you are
As you belittle your inner self with scores equaling as pars
That silver screen
Hollywood lights
Always put their audience in a state of awe
The plane goes nearly aloof despite all the past flights
Who has custody of my private thought
Nearly sheared brains with their mega amount of cells
Back in high school I just slipped past
Holes in the cement cracks
Everybody whispered-he is smart yet something he lacks
Now times do change
Matter of fact
They certainly do
Aligned inertia's do motivate
And with their accuracy redirect a failing crew
Illustrated conceptions sometimes find their own fault
Just like being at a zoo
Come on in and listen to the music
That resonates from a nearly cartoon rock band
During this glimpse of time and what is best
Renew your zeal
With some needed and deserved rest

WRITTEN BY: Brian Moilanen 2013

Insomnia's Insensibility

Defective drama
Possibly incorporates retrieval of
That which is sometimes nearly irreversible
Yet what is strikingly effective is to define
The durable elective
Sleeping pills
Without opportunity or chance for a good chance of restful sleep
Chronic
Abnormally prolonged
As for essential necessity I erratically of the cheated folk
And what is attached is sleeplessness that focuses upon the wrong
A favorable supposed cure is to find a tub and warmly soak
I do not have the position of a favorable hero
When abounded with all attributes although
I minimally escape the targeted shots of being a perilous zero
Look at me face to face
My eyes are blood shot and torn
And appear as if symmetrically out of place
Circumspect
Before you attempt to land a rude shot
Is it judge or prejudge
An item or pretense-did I fit in your gaming slot
Tragic or is it not
With no effort to analyze any effect only upon me
A suggestion or preposterous idea
Not being self- centered, should I run or swiftly flea
Overpower the careless-And weed out them out
Such as the armed forces
This is what the remembering soul contains and is all about
With your claim despite aversion of your problem
Learn to develop a masterpiece of new intention
Dignity of lives completeness
Venerable yet still without magnetic intention
Without penalty for freedom of speech let my standards
Find your trivialized heart without apprehension
I am feeling recovery
Downright sober and lowly
Yet inward seeing and finding discovery
Claiming up to an hour or two of sleep
That is for the whole complete day
An infection
That through the cracks goes without detection
Light shining back to light
Call it harvested refection
Chasing the dragon
Yet I certainly no
I do not need an artificial sentiment
The dark side-may it be called vile
Is tricky-and can trick and deceive as a way to represent and resent
Should I repent
Learn
Earn
Find and locate benediction while beginning again to pray
Can I be formed as puttying held down
Or that of manipulated hand held clay
Insomnia
It has the know-how to transform
Yet usually not outperform
Please keep me at the societal norm
Insomnia-deal with it
Insomnia-or it will deal with you

54

Intention of Intimacy

Spacious-wide-and all-inclusive
My intent of this desired nearness is beyond far stretched
Difficult for my own mind to comprehend currently-seeing this as elusive
My goals-Those near and yet intriguing dreams
If you would prefer-let your ears hear them as….
My forthright intent-my objective-precisely how it seems
Perceptions
Where are you now-without compelling attitude
Receptions
Do you evenly understand my brains elevation-all reversible revelation
An understanding of my lives course
Pacified and earthly-all retribution given at my time of conception
A big hand given-larger than life and life itself
Look back to those characteristic years-observe the reflection
Do you categorize into e.s.p.-or even beyond prying stealth
In need
In desperation-upon and at its given times
Listen to the church bells sounding
Can you hear almost oppressed yet ultimately desired church chimes
Intimacy
Beit with lover-love-or request of joys understanding
Hear from this prophets poor-yet subtle voice
Alone again conceding although with my hearts demanding
Reprimanding
Answering the call to God about sin and regarded mistake
With minimal exception
Turning from what others-simply lie back and distrusted-do not forsake
Yet-besides this error
And mistake I make-mans view
May lead to silent inner terror-yet God above will renew
And make you cleansed-as new
Sleep like a baby tonight-with my lady in my arms
In hopes that you enjoy the gold and silver locket
That on which the inside-is filled with reddened heart charms
My intent
Is never-although pinnacle-never void or spent
I value the prominent yesterdays
And shall see what the distant tomorrows have specified and lent
I do frequently repent
I aim to-stay on track
Please forgive me
If too much time with myself was inanimately spent
Introspection's
If you do the math
Is it all-even though current and fresh-all mind retention
Maybe
Maybe not
What counts the most
Is this aversion towards light-You gave your best shot
WRITTEN BY: BRIAN MOILANEN 2010

It's Going to Be Worth It

Financially
Money being so tight-it's as the skin on a hot air balloon
Mentally
I am not curbing my current sadness and will not play your wet eyed buffoon
Faithfully
I have my mustard seed and am ready to knock down that gigantic mountain
Physically
I am in shape somewhat by choice-yet mainly diplomatic and tough discipline
Sentimentally
Tender feelings thru time-harden me yet not so as to routine sin
Emotionally
Torn in two and pondering deep-with ways to succeed as a whole-a gathered win
Going with and amongst a slump-how to wear a legitimate grin
The roof around me appears to be falling in over my head
The tunnel I crawled inn too escape is-literally caving right in
Shocked while tantalized-I think I am being detained
My inner voice is doing its screaming and yelling
Significance of this ongoing situation being severely pained
And in vertigo I see myself habitually dwelling
I-to this purpose
Have seen the light at the end of the tunnel over a hundred times
Yet occasionally still stock up on lemons
Because I profusely became burned out on the limes
Can and do you understand-most men are and become brutish by their own knowledge
Saps like that learn their lesson beit hard knocks or college
How to rightfully instruct
Where and when vile evil deems so impartial-not taught in sneered college
How to rightfully instruct
When evil turns strangely against evil and is beyond corrupt
What stems that violent caged volcano
Inside the poverty stricken hands-and though even angel possibility could erupt
In time-and time alone
Things will change-readily they will and shall
Balance carries the person upon the creaky bridge
And not necessarily the guiding hand rail
Wear someone else clothes-and not to mention shoes
For desperation through paid efforts
Could bring even Santa Clause-along with elves-to their dispersed blues
Take a stand
Lend a guiding hand
Fulfilling to God-answering from the King
Would never overly discipline-yet still understand quality and command
Think it over-there is more to life than the you
For it is going to get better-doors open
I will gladly show you thru

WRITTEN BY: BRIAN MOILANEN

The Unknown–Day of Reckoning

End of calendars
End of years-henceforth this is the end of days
Minutes appear ensconced-and now wind down
The world is abruptly being enrolled and has
No tomorrow and actually nothing much more left
Envisioning either the beginning of the day of atonement
Or if 4 leaf clovers will blossom and we are still to be fortunate
Not much more than the breaking and busting of one of the seals
This is a duty and privilege of mine-which I hold and manifest
Oceans waters are not challenged as of yet-still colored teal-another final test
God must reign until he hath put all enemies under his feet
Is it possible to convert one million agnostics along with their non believers
Will God please hear me-as I with game plan-have openly confessed
Or is it truly worldly-too late
God will violently avenge-and weeks prior
Shall with destruction contained wrath-completely demonstrate
It is not only Israel cut off from the true Messiah
But surprisingly the entire world has lost all special favor
The grand finale is beginning to advent
With what I only assume-tear drops to savor
The day of the Lord
What if my hands are those
That hold that mighty Godly sword
I must keep up with these biblical teachings as keynote
Of God's holy-fair-just and kind most respectable Holy Word
For our knowledge-The Almighty has more names
More names than just….King of kings and Lord of lords
Also 16 other Old testament names-even names such as….Shalom
Which means-The Lord is my peace
The church before has been my refuge and home
And by sentiment it is my faith through release
Back to the subject at hand
Will on this day the 1rst seal be opened and the final battle begin
Or merely the 7th seal be opened and worked from within
Through sentiment near in the future-There will be one final shocking revelation
The sanctification
Explaining a vindication
That supremely Jehovah is ruler of this creation
And that his obedient tried son Jesus-is ruler over all creation
And that beside Israel Christianity is practiced throughout every nation
This is my true remedying proclamation
That releases its own type of sustenance
Times on this earth get tough-as nails
Yet never as wicked-as the horrors of hell
Remember this before you sleep
And to that-even before you awake
For God does allow-thought attached to destiny
For God does not exist in that permanent penalty those being the fiery lake
Observe the almighty angel-before I am forgotten
Remember that ordained holy apple from Genesis
For through it all-it had never became rancid or rotten

WRITTEN BY: BRIAN MOILANEN 2010

Just Another Number

Daily these vegetables are pulled from the earth's climate based of earth
Yet maybe nothing more than a lavished cucumber
Welcome to this land of plantings of importance or not-For this beit is the amassed earth
And although distinguished somehow-you are just another number
Do I sound to cynical
Or am I speaking downright truth-pervasive of any lie
I was told a saying such as this at a young age
And it still holds somewhat true-that much I cannot deny
What is the world's population
My estimation of reports says that of about 4.6 billion
And If we were all seedlings-I would still stand tall and plant myself firm
Push out those devastation causing worries of grief and detriment to grow
Yet I see these rudiments of hazard-the increments of the roots of a germ
And they are able to paralyze-and decrease the chance to flow-a chain of life that could slow
Yet with billions around-what am I to my enemies and their numbers also
It all reflects upon what is inside each of these vegetables
Call them cucumbers-or whatever so
These numbers
Enormous and not always so swift
Still their seeds get planted
And get rooted amongst the rains subtle nightly
Yet all of these
Amongst and within the midst
Are all exactly numbered
Such as the fingers-in an iron clad fist
What is your number
What is my number
Many times I consider myself a blessed number 13
Ousted with severe problems at times-yet like Houdini
Always escape with my life abundant and healthy-can you see what I mean
Something tells me-you-yes you
Might be a number 4
Outstretched arms cling for another success in which to cling
And to hold
Your heart does with oration speak and overtly sing
Or a product of its environment in which you must mold
The numbers with attached names-do collectively talk
Nightmares are in desperate waiting although
Dormant-and ready to negotiate a horrific scare of body or mind
Don't think about this dilemma more than twice
And the only rewind-Is in which the great days relived and ready to find
Keep in mind
Numbers is the mass sum of all that surrounds
Add it all up
And you will locate complacency that dumbfounds
Numbers
We are all given one
Does it comprise your life
Are you at all having fun

WRITTEN BY: Brian Moilanen 2013

Logistics of Love

What is your visual perception and understanding
Of the delicacy of the true word as we call it love
Resurrection of the soul to my immediate surroundings
Yet also nearing that unforeseen usually known place as vertigo
Yet speculation leads to comprehension that this
Is not an unreasonable out of body experience
Yet I do feel quite odd although being as a preeminent
As if I were rich and a nobleman.....my God as a lowly prince
A phenomenal anthem to the exotic
If I am dreaming...let me know
For separation of fact to fiction is still quite neurotic
Don't worry partner....or should I call you friend
Love is passion within enclosed compassion
And it is a drag when it does end
Genuine love
Love that surpasses all factors-opposite of being a phony
Where is the transcending
Flight of the Pegasus neighbors itself that of the pony
A winged horse to be exact
I make an effort to ponder prior to proliferation
That is a sure bet to decrease
Foot in mouth disease and mental deterioration
There are different types of love although
Some that last eternally
And others just materially
Divide the cards
Split the deck
Both are reversals of goal
Yet both equal....goals of reversal
Like during a play at the theater
When do you separate fact from fiction
Or do you at all
Just a living contradiction
Just loving to love
Yes....reach for the stars
If you pledge to reach high enough
You might stand and have depth far enough to even touch....Mars
Everyday logic supplies everything else we bring to our surrounding world
Animals, earth, fish and beast
All of which is entirely important
And of this series-none of which compares being the least
Without love the antecedent develops and grows as sickening
And honestly enough only compounds and squanders as it also dumbfounds
Sure we all have times where we dislike, anger and even hate
Yet let it never let it lowly or for that matter-deeply rule
O situations can get brutal, uneducated and quite irate
So stop with the teasing belief
And wipe clean the slate
Love has taught me that each day brings a brand new chance
Dancing with the angels
An indelible dance contained with soft romance
You see-each day births its elements for another beginning
Arbitration's of money are important yet not everything
In any case of peace and not calamity-see yourself as winning

59

How do you see the logistics of love
Quite seriously
Speaking in the land of logistics how do you calculate love
Maybe you truly do not
And for that matter-maybe I truly don't
For love can't be seen
But in observation-loves actions can
With effort-We are all on God's team
If we stick to an Almighty plan
Love and be loved-to name one of the few
I don't have the ability to market myself as the creator of rules
Such as you-one who is in school
Laboring intensely-And not a hooligan or one of the fools

WRITTEN BY: BRIAN MOILANEN

Lost and Not Found

I am lost
Screaming in desperation-can someone please find me
Tangling with what is corrupt
That of a blazing volcano
Which spews red heated anger
Downward I channel with vertigo and soon solemnly will erupt
I review my wasted time-including both day and night
An unsettled perplexed feeling
Growing deeper is my anguish bordering on a horrific sight
Trapped
Yes trapped
And now falling into a hellish abyss
Glancing back at the earth
Those time were minimal and gosh how I do miss
Clearly I modify to this caged electric jungle
Lost and also not yet found
An alien ant farm
Insects of differing species perplexed on a muddied dirt mound
Who am I
And beyond that just what are you
Caged ballistic gorillas
Trapped deeply within a human zoo
Vast safaris include their biological equal
If my life terminates now
Bet your bottom dollar that you will see a sequel
Is time against me-it appears as if so
Melancholy I just can't deny
Is this hell
If so-why should I even try

WRITTEN BY: Brian Moilanen 2013

Love Search

Evidently running out of hate
And climbing into a secured love
Cleverly a new hand will find you
And it is preserved within this yellow glove
Now using love to overcome the adversary-known as hate
Which possibly is fashioned as merely circumstantial
Overwhelmed with consequences of actions-I become quite irate
Allowing warmth, affection, and joy to
Fervently and abundantly grow
Harnessing my outcome as sentimental emotion
Interested I watch as this celestial light-begins now and does glow
I drift in my boat-neighboring between shore and ocean
Hmm...what remains hidden sometimes does show
Uniquely this sensation gives freedom an ultimatum of chance
Within my body I now have a heart of gold
Zoning in on this state of mentality I sing and dance
Upon this ocean I count each infinite mile
As I wish for holy angels dwelling near-an ear to lend
Lives thread interlocks days-while attaining to night's dusk
Methodology seeks divinity-a serendipitous bend
Currently I subliminally shop for newer frontiers
Uniquely a manifestation of soul yet without tears
No more fears
Or bigoted sarcasm resulting in shunning-call that jeers

WRITTEN BY: Brian Moilanen 2013

Love-Struck Romantic

The cheese-playfully attached moves via the energetic string
Although standing-I feel as if in praise of prayer
Creditably noted upon bowed and bended knees
Yet will I gainfully seize this prey consisting of aromatic cheese
Yet I see this situation in a much different aspect
Will this figuratively end in a catch of complete necessity
Or reckon that of the past-a poster boy of cruel neglect
Now I am merely attracted to what is acceptably right
This equilibrium tick tocks and winds up at at 12-the number composed of respect
Because even though I am just one
My faults of existing-prosper with her equivalent as two
Never-mind this mind- fulfilled enchantment of just….
What is what
Who is this she-supposedly part of a diverse picture
Will she-my girlfriend of fiction and not fact
Ever become as with me being attached-that of a fixture
I still have not received that heaped reward
That reward being cheese….or a lover….duplicity within does revolve
Will I find a religious woman-a believer
And not just a digging tool-someone who claims that we did evolve
The cheese still moves haphazardly as those intrigued with magic
The mouse is ready to pounce on its target
With both the end and the beginning-seemingly now-not as tragic
I do genuinely have sufficient love remaining in soul and heart
I will do anything legal for my so called….ace of spades
Whoops-I stand corrected as I almost lied
Because I will omit a game reverent of charades
And stay totally aware of an evil world-yet with its hint of joy
If I were an auctioneer
Instead of these games-could I buy you top-dollar as a toy
Games concurrent with life
Yes-all people do play
Yea-yea-It although makes me internally sick
Watch me-As I might just cough up this coupling nasty phlegm
Put down your peace pipe
I shall utmost-do the same
Never did I imagine I would finish 2nd to last
In this game of love/hate debacle-we both play this game
I would quit If I could
Then just get swallowed by its lethal competition
I although always-yes always-with her love remain in this expedition
Jovial-tremendous fulfillment of fun times
Life a journey
Jaunt
Venture
All the qualities a couple should explicitly want
Someday I will catch that elusive cheese
And get on with my lives excursion
Travel the world or meekly purchase a frugal house
Because sometimes it is you who is catching
And it is me who has been deemed the mouse

WRITTEN BY: BRIAN MOILANEN 2010

Mental and Maddening Mind Game

Am I blessed or oddly gist and more enduring with added stress
Wind me up and watch me forwardly go
Cantankerous while attached to what is abashed-My mind frame merely does guess
I feel drunk-as if in a stupor-although sources report as not
Deja-vu....or is my mind up to its cunning tricks
Obloquy has found a resting home-a resting spot
Mechanics of the mind are also yet not deserving upon daily game
What would I do if I had a million
And each bill of money-knew me by name
Would that change ego-mind-and they way in which the cards were dealt
Emotion undermines sentiment-therefore accompanied with solace-heartache to find me
All of these feelings conceivable-all are now being felt
Hush-hush
Shh...take reason and considered time to think
I am in control
As this white paper consolidates character in the form of ink
The rivers are running low in elevation and tide
As another dream does sink
Or maybe cuts through the madness-with monumental success on the brink
As said...
To every action there is an equal and positive reaction
How can this be true although for example
When someone is brain-dead with body nearly unmovable-and in traction
Think about it-whatever it is
And will it think about you
Turn the screw
Tighten the clasped end with glue
Throwing dice
High dice total equals victory
Are certain occasions better than others
Hold on to your applicable ace card-wait and just see
Shortest straw
The highest and best suit of cards
Sinking only the solids-with 8 ball in the corner pocket
How can I pedal this bike
When most of its teeth have resigned-and fall off the sprocket
Throwing darts
Scores equaling nil at win of chance
Today is not your day partner
Twisted degrees are added to their circumstance
Destined to....I just cants
Or am I not quite sure
Watch despite this maddening bad luck streak-or slump
You will win this battle 2 fold-and get over that rapidly diminishing hump
Watch the blazing motorcycles
Where would they be-if they could not jump
Or when offset in the mind-is it only because they are at a stump
My offense of concealing my days that hurt awfully bad
I may have been toyed with or indolent
But I never-I repeat never have been had

WRITTEN BY: BRIAN MOILANEN 2010

Moreover a 1000 or More Tears

The day was going great and bidding to be one of fine recollect
Then the horrific news of grimness hit me harder than a ton of bricks
I realized I had lost a dear loved one
And within the truth of situation it caused its brutal conflicts
How could this happen
How and why today
The sun of 9o degrees began to grow transparent and lifeless
Even the luminous yellowing turned to a frail black like gray
A loss of thought not to mention feeling
Onward although I did cry for….
God's purity and loving sacred healing
What to do
And for that matter just what to say
My conscious teams up with my soul
And begs for my physical body to stay
My dear friend of long
Had passed this earth in favor without doubt
Yet why so soon
I now questioned what the meaning of life was all about
Tears canvassed my face as if it were a painting without admittance of referral
Even if it were a black cold night
My weeping's could be seen- as if nocturnal
Death, disease, famine and shame
All concordances of the dark side
And defiant of the key word titled fame
I feel alone
Nothing quite honestly right now seems to matter
Yet invisibly he is one step nearer to God
And his steps were upon God's ladder
Climb high
Climb so high where at the current you cannot be seen
Flooding me with fond memory
And I feel as if I have landed in a pile of financial green
Not that this money matters at all
Yet it can pay my bills and allow for monumental thrills
Despite as if a needle in a haystack
I managed to locate a holy bible within this pile of what almost appears as abundant as leaves
My friend found heaven and that is for sure
Or is he waiting dead and unknowing waiting for Christ's second return
I silence myself beside the tears and sorrow
As somehow a slight smirk draws itself upon an empty face
Did this day truly occur today
Or was I just readying myself
As if I were playing lead in a Hollywood play
Praise God
Give laud to friend and family
Do not forget yourself
As you emotionally and plainly see

WRITTEN BY: BRIAN MOILANEN

<u>My Truth is My Life's Resume!</u>
Tricks play fond within this delicate mind
Am I a noble-a noble nothing
Only saturated with a sophisticated brain in which you will find
Poor me a drink of red wine
I will play by the rules
And at the moment-am feeling quite fine
Only a few dimes and one nickel to hold
Kicked out of diners for vacuity-I believe despite not of my own fault
I guess that I fit into the mulish mold
Never one to brag or boast
Maybe I should not even think that way of reaching a summit
Yet If not
Will my life or joy-begin to plummet
An I.Q. of 110 is well above average
That of which I do comfortably mold
I always attempt in the spiritual warfare of life to be fair
Represent care
And not dare the mentally or spiritually defunct
For if doing so
Misfortune at a later date-could find my career junked
Pray
To a God
Or thee God
Do I make you ill or slightly sick in a good reverence
Run over by a 20 mile per hour freight train
I lived
Rolled a car 4 times at 70 miles per hour
I lived
Put me at a pond in Florida in the heat of summer in hopes of gold
I sieved and strained
Only fool's gold
Yet still-not even that one was lost
I am honest and oh so real
Genuinely zeal
A unique and enchanting feel
I came to this land to win and not to lose
Life-liberty-and the pursuit of happiness
God bless you-followed up by a distant 2nd placed subjugated me
Life is now-live it wisely and not fret about spending an extra buck
I have earned integrity and just cannot lose
I have that-7 leaf clover luck
Somewhat green-opposite of mean
That is-if you know what I mean
Not to mention
Played in some rock bands that hit the charts-
thru and by the underground
I have even spoken with David Koresh-told him too wait
He felt his followers were at the end
When all they had to do was mend
Not pretend
Lend
For those Branch Davidian's were at the top of the heap
And jumping out of heaven
Was never and wasn't the intended leap-only a leap of faith!
WRITTEN BY: BRIAN MOILANEN-2010

66

Narrowly You Although-Enter the Gate

Possibly by assured redemption
The forgiveness of transgressions
Inevitably is marked by all of your absolution-with exception
Mostly for method of logic transferred
And taken in those later years of your exercised new course of action
Yes-you became a Christian late in life
Even though late-the decision you made is recanted to that of a quality reaction
Yet we all should understand that keeping the faith is difficult
In a world that demands more than just ourselves-it also demands a true heart
An influenced moral stand and ethics included
Do not barge self- righteously into others lives persistently
You in the long run
May find that you are then not included
Although a laymen and a regular Joe he was so to say
Your actions and accompanied deeds prove that you are not that small
The function of mind in relation to its obtaining information
Sometimes is previously already nearly known
You allowed yourself late in life to flourish
Wow...what you have patch worked and mightily sown
Your spirit and attitude was exemplified by God via Christ
And nearly began to become that of a small movement
Did I illicitly holler-can you take a hint
As for me
I turned to God at a young age
Took to the notorious stage-and renovated my peers with
Contentment-which as you know is refreshing-and unlike rage
Not perfect-far from it as the earth to the sun
Yet following Christ and doing good and what is Godly
Has its discretion-and can be a heck of a lot of fun
Make it a goal not to see how much you are able to sin
Yet turn from sin and bondage
The heavens above will count it all up and include even me-in the win
Do not ever vanquish the poor for they way they are
Or what they do or do not have
For in God's eyes if faithful and fertile-they may be his focused meek star
Be careful
Yet be pure
For as the poor-your time of need will come I promise you
And how you treated the others-even if not in sin
The right choices within you from the past have furtively grew
Give someone a break even if struggling or wrong
This is maybe not a poem
For it neighbor itself that of a Psalm

WRITTEN BY: BRIAN MIOILANEN 2010

Nice Guys Finish Last

Currently-I am in last place
Not even a close 2nd-information I need to provide
Nice guys finish last-such as that statement which explains that old adage
Is there anyone who maintains with this side
If so-we will lecture one another upon the value of success
And its many ways-as we furnish for that piteous car ride
Of course-I have gave and been given to alike
I chase always after victory-even in its simplistic form
If a had feathered wings-would I be considered a nike
And a soul enduring schism-is this a human problem-what others consider the norm
Ask yourself this
If the masses of population-continue to financially grow
Why is it-despite my only riches-being of the mind
That practically nothing seems to flow-and imminently forwardly go
Grievance
Detriment-not also to forget to mention pained
Tarnished and branded
Did I nearly forget to mention-stained
What merits a lucky plan of rescue
Tongue-tied and nearly exhausted
What appears plausible-or just redesign my game plan as new
Fortunes-money
Riches and wealth
Did I already analyze my main problem
Being too open-I receive a grade of a d-, when it comes to stealth
Maybe moreover-I need to study firmly my inner being
Do I play my shuffled deck of cards correctly or adept and wise
The poll I did is complete-and with my understanding-people are very agreeing
I give and typically others do take
Yet the flow and transmission of goods with brains concur
And I quite honestly-am not that deceiving ancient clever snake
If your idea of me involves that-than I shall immediately with obtuse just defer
Some ignorance's steal
Some sufferings only lead to heartache
Some are at the top-as they reach the summit
And the minority of followers-seem trivial and return only once again to plummet
Shift into overdrive
Save your fuel in this journey or escapade
For if you are not secure and wisely play
Your empire of sheer monotony-is unguarded-and enemies could raid
Be ready
Stay steady
For as a promise from almighty God
You will soon open gifts-and toss aimless the confetti
For even as there or seem to be
Stay in tune-not with radio or television
Yet with yourself
Which mirrors itself as a picture of you-imposed as me

WRITTEN BY: BRIAN MOILANEN 2010

No Man's Land-Part #2

Apparently
Not much need for all of this once portentous geographically wasted space
Mankind is diverging and purging
Yet this plan of action only allows for us to numbly erase
Just what is common-place
And where beyond that-did it go
Standard operational procedures
Only find the waste bucket can-as I begin to primitively throw
Is this World War #III
Peace protesters of all culture-type and kind
The canvass of this story seems to be prearranged
And all of the lead characters being countries of war-are aligned
People and families protest the near the White House as change they came to see
This war of nations and country alike
Yet there is not enough unbiased support
To sway those indifferent
To the doubting for a remedy-which actually would pose as a strike
All of this infliction
Does it not market itself-as a contradiction
It truly is a world- wide affliction
Changing of the tide
Who are your allies-who is your colleague in this game of war
Even families without weapons or a formal military service
Fight with ink on paper-nearly as strong as the core
When will the American soldiers reach the muddied and wet shore
The years of enlistment now will probably reach more than 4
Years of service that is
Who is the mastermind of this aggression-what is next in this to explore
Tanks move and are on their quick 35- mile per hour run
Flattening everything within its way or path
With the missiles being fired-can you see their cataclysmic wrath
Just a never-ending body count of immensity now
Resentment built anger has led to another loss-another bloodbath
Is there a chance for peace and disposition
A reconciliation's chance of….leave us be
Soldiers
They become a dozen to a dime
Or is it-a dime to a dozen
A problem that branches out fluidly
And if superimposed is actually a cause from within
Which leads to another scenario of effortless chagrin
Bondage and sin
Despite-you must play to win
When and if possible in combat-wear an adulated grin
Like a well shot portrait-the skies will light up
A fourth of July nightly paraded show
All the honor
With this collusion-it creates a glazed lightning glow
No man's land
I will despite-keep on giving to my country in every way
In a land currently-that is anxious to take
I despite this trying time-will not give up
And not abandon or even ever think of putting into forsake
WRITTEN BY: BRIAN MOILANEN

Nothing Today Makes Any Sense

The future
What is in store
I will hold on
To see what is there too explore
The past
How much of it drags on by
Before you compliantly recognize
And wonder why
That without rhyme or reason
It will always whisper to us….goodnight and goodbye
No one is able to technically relive it physically
I also understand the never-ending pursuit of wish-going to glory
Yet that will not be-at least maybe not to be kicked off metaphysically
How much although of it-if we could-return to by chance
Probably that enchanting romance of yesteryear-how cathartic
I mentally relive that moment and recall that one time perfect slow dance
Cursed out cussed out-by their impervious imperfections
You see it your way-in turn-I will see it mine and inwardly plow
Psychosis-neurosis-depression
Multiple personality-schizophrenia-all these attributions are also the outsiders anomaly
Paranoia projects
Fictions figments of apparently very near fear
Pushing or rolling certain objects-tanks or reef
I can see it everywhere in small substance
I understand the grief
Call up your higher power
And let it thus
Never give in-never to cower
Joy-a brand new toy
Which whom does this comfortably employ
Girl or boy
Boy or girl-watch her and her amazing blond curl
Still one of God's living creatures
Yet to the overly rich snobbish ones
Deemed a monster or worse-as seen on daily rhetoric cartoon features
Stay tuned
Welcome to the good guy-and add that-O
I will gladly hotly fill up
Your awaiting cup of black joe
Do you not know
The blowing winds represent the wins
And I am stable and secure
And in subtle form-am inside a bucket of penguins-followed with the grins
Am I clay
Which you in turn-help to mold
Day after day
An image
A likeness of you trapped in this carcass of humbled confusion
Or is this-and am I….
Just an illusion
I say hello to others
You-with no recognition or response
Do I exist
Yet I must
The cars fly past
And the breeze displays all of their exhaust

WRITTEN BY: BRIAN MOILANEN 2010

Of Sanctity and Sentiment

Remarkably as I do see it
A gratified soul cavorts being solemn and righteous
Which forwardly moves into a colored creativity
And acknowledges as proper and a litigator of truth
Off goes the heavy and mixed mask
Without blinders-a time in which to truly see
Trudging strenuously that extra long mile
Okay
Even possibly going the extra foot or two
Winners that lead acquire a tempered devotion
While only obtained by the diligent some
Yet much further than an entitled few
Destiny of desire-watch as joy begins to steadily run
Always locate a trail of desire which alludes uncertainty
Lead us to Christ-God's most perfect holy son
As innocent goes the verdict-along with its plea
While ultimately trying to forget
Undeserved pain and societal neglect
Not allowing for technicality-To grow as regret
Comfort and release-time to create a new friend
A tightly wrapped precious gift from Jehovah God
So many new and good tidings
Yet not enough time remains on planet earth
A compassionate integrity is what is left to send

WRITTEN BY: Brian Moilanen 2013

One Chilly Cold Night

One chilly cold night
I called you my dearest friend
Talking about good times
And how they won't ever end
A game of cards
We laugh and drink beer
I miss your smiling face
How I wish that you were here
Sharing almost the same mind
Flowing this game with caution we both agreed
Identity inspiring what is the need to find
And planting the infinite Christian seed
Separation concluded now by time and space
Depths of similarity
This being a void that I cannot just erase
Gathering rays of light determined by this galaxies sun
Frolic was this fabric-a friendship conceding as needlework
A philosophy of pertinence that says to get it done
Rock bands and cigarette breaks
Following up as mysterious intervention
Allowing for fantasy and all the drive it takes
Honesty destroys an uncomfortable tension
Fantasy was first and reality as secondary
Not quitting ever-even if everybody else did
Abstaining from burning out and also being wary
A cold drink as a temporary solution
And yes it is-the conflict of human nature and just how to rid
But now things are different
People have changed
Looking forward now
Pieces of this puzzle uniquely have rearranged
To relive the past-sometimes we all do
Finding the right chord along with rhyme too
Promoting efforts to cling
And seeing each day as brand new

Written by: Brian Moilanen 2013

<u>One Too Many</u>
Mistakes
Errors
Misguided directives
Pay attention now to the improvising electives
Count to add up in order the totality of sequence of events
And then do the guesswork-which will formulate as subjective
I have made many mistakes
Upon and after being skilled at an art or profession
Productivity subsequently finds itself neighboring with solidity
Examples or just merely a wandering mind
Favoring subliminal sanctions that are set to free
The torments of it all- most do run to a certain spot
Freedom usually equals true escape when worries grow nil and void
I need a sub-sample at ways for another chance
So therefore-do not become the authority of being annoyed
Or one that has subscribed to being unjustly toyed
Yes-I have failed at missions being of the same
Yet in hindsight
See the indifference's as borderline and thus claiming as sane
Yet altogether the sum is always chasing pain
Running from all this heartache I have became as in a stupor
3 strikes and you are out
Where has went the dispensation
These days it is just word without origin or creation
Where is minor joy deemed as love or as an allocation
A creation with and without substantiation
A deaf ears nu-found proclamation
Yet with stern input remotely is barely heard
Fouled up by an outsiders grievances
I feel as if these efforts are obscured
Ignorance of a prospecting corridor
Can you locate those words that have cured
Falling down
Taking the fall
A dead corpse that is in a coffin
Is laid out in a formed sprawl
Yet-I am not a dead man
I have diligently learned
Moreover I have fought
The yesterdays have transcribed
In all facets these variables have taught
For I did not come into this world to lose or give up
Spring up on those young legs being mild and pliant
Tiny Labrador pup
Same as myself
Trace the steps despite your young age
Do not let conflict of interest cause
Pessimism, intolerance or deep-seated rage
Quiet your temper
Let lose of all 53 emotions
Yet keep intact with those 7 base feelings
Choose your temperament as it chooses you
Jump across the hoops
As it is a measure of chronological succession
Defeating yet meeting-and collaborating with any and all groups

Only a Dollar More

Do you ever feel as if in a state of complete abeyance
This a shoppers world-catering so to say to the richly divine
Both feeling deflationary yet also genuine-now subsequent and untimely
You must be although able to recognize this red flagged sign
Instead of saving a buck
Maybe this would abduction of the soul
Remembering what was blamelessly bought
Yet what was crudely stole
Probably you should think this one out
And strive for a foundation of at least a moderate thrill
Spend a dollar more
Make sure to serve yourself and your disquieted host
Yet do not subject to pompous intuition
And settle for an ungodly cost-and become as toast
Squeeze yourself for a momentary cure
As our time on this ambiguous world is seemingly short
Even the wisest of minds would agree-and testify as sure
Treat your friend or family or those that are near
Sometimes when thinking back to the best
Awestruck-sometimes all you do is ponder with and stare
Re-claim those days
That without doubt you targeted as great
Comfort with cordiality
Do you think you have passed the test
What test you may add
The test of having fun
Whether in the rain or in the sun
So follow your heart
And...get er' done
Money
Do you follow the rich or the poor
Sometimes...what does it matter
And exactly what is in the auctioneer's store
Yes you have saved still while having spent
Put your percentages in the tithe bowl
The process and action of having of had to repent
Of course you have passed the dollar to the cashier
At times-you have grossly overspent
Not always pennies in the penny bank
Where do all those cents go-where have they went
The scent
The scene
Feeling quite obscure and odd
As randomly you find a suitcase of lost cash-behind the bushy ravine
Now you know what it is too have a wallet full -a fat wad
Got lucky
Luck found you
Bewildered and contagious
Now-just what should I do

WRITTEN BY: BRIAN MOILANEN 2010

Pallid Places

Strangely lacking in color
Because of this lack of substance contained
The situation and its fixtures-only get duller and duller
Pallid places
Abstinence nearly fleas from the colors that as it chases
Urban faces
The minority either keeps or erases
Time amongst time itself- almost as if playing charades
Walk in desperation yet keeping in stride with its paces
These moments with its responsibilities has although a love conquer
A way to last through my existence of this life
Things and of what plans should mightily endure
As mentioned-not to be skeptical or renounced
Yet if this were tennis we were playing
Me as the ball-could be sidelined and jounced
Mostly altruistic I aim to be
Yet as though a god-I am capable despite of being badly hurt and that much more
I usually feel as a number-and add up just the same
Which probably is the spoil to any war
When money is tight I am a number 13
Yet when securing it and spending it
Others from every corner and even in-between see me as potential green
Look at those colors to be precise-lack there of
The cold of events such as this is remarkable
I see that you found of mine a glove
The earth we live in
Is splendid with all colors in which to speak
Opposite of some of the mainstay of arbitration's voice
With luck anyway-may just speak to the meek
We need some red
We also need some black and white
Although lacking at times
There must be a way for them to universally unite
Do we need more or less people to line this planet of divided wealth
O.K.
Skip the wealth and focus on health
For it is better to be broke and have a voice
Then to be broken and with millions-yet no voice endearing concerns at all
My love for my girlfriend is much and means more than a ton of bricks
She guides me through the social dilemmas
Even gave me a nice crucifix
Yet how do I get my kicks
Not being off-color
Playing it right-innuendo intended
Catching a person's lie
Without cuffs-I am able to reprimand and make them mentally apprehended

WRITTEN BY: BRIAN MOILANEN 2010

Playing Life's Cards

A seemingly broken life-garbled and in manifested shambles
This perpetuates and surrounds its own shadow
Chemistry somehow contained within suggestive doubt-it with acuity rambles
Far from mirth or given good will
Just as if back-peddling
To get up this seeming never-ending hill
Yet I am getting closer to my small cottage home
Although as it feels I have been in between
Here and methodologically the vast expanse of Rome
Too many bills-People to pay
A reputation though that is known as perfectly fair
Should I imposingly be in self-discernment
And rationalize with-I really currently do not care
A piece of mind
Within my ways exacts itself as...
A peace of mind
Yet beside all of the hustle and bustle
A slave to the grind
Yet I know this jagged puzzle piece will fit
And requirement of will adhere to a pictorial and visual find
See the big picture
Do not quit
Even while striding evidently way ahead
Remember -if it exists
The pain of the poor mans dread
Bequeathed and handed down a hand
Good or bad
Maybe impartial and stuck as in...indifferent
Yet-we are taught by nature and God to play
Sometimes we become lost in the ethics of ethics
And our brain grows slumber-utter dismay
IS life taken with relative ease
Or is it a tough competition that is not so simple
I see sometimes your face smile
Wow….what a cute dimple
Whether you disagree and seem congruous
You may hunt me- I may add
But you can only harm and not kill this moose
In life
I have wronged
And in turn my soul and conscience play tricks
Some people over-ride these wrong doings
And inwardly only get their own kicks
Play your cards
And not reverse of order
Even if I was a dwarf or midget
You ironically would be the one who is shorter
Think the stars
Push for the moon
Find satire when need be
And as a classic lesson-we all occasionally play the buffoon

WRITTEN BY: BRIAN MOILANEN

Please Forgive Me

Such as you
I have transgression's that are laden with mistakes
I attempt to see holy angels
Yet is appears that-you just and only see snakes
At times I was seen with open eyes
Yet often times now these eyes do close
If time grows knowledge-am I therefore wise
Recalculating my game plan
Within confidence I climb higher and choose to revise
Although another slammed door-tail between my legs
If I am wrong-please remove these crucifix's aching pegs
Yes Christ is the Godhead and central to human nature
Then why do you label with the attached tags
Please forgive me
As I have many times forgiven others
A plan of joyous comfort that bonds and unites
And Jehovah God notices us as sisters and brothers
The body and spirit collide with conscious and spirit
Although you are planets away
God's plan if followed is supreme-can you hear it
My unfailing eyes
An angels sweet kiss and dreams abound
Angels often whisper
Yet with noise are splendidly found
Halos
Divinity
Saintly and moving
For only those medically blind to see
Talk to formulate your opinion
We know although sometimes talk is cheap
Don't risk your value with heaven
And consoling comfort is what you will reap
Please forgive
Attempt to forget
If adventure is a game
Then forthright I understand you will win the bet

Written by: Brian Moilanen 2013

Pour Me a Drink

Human behavior
Sometimes an enigma of the sort that ends in ridiculous rhyme
She eats whole tart lemon
While I resort to the likes of a robust lime
A concoction of the two-yet they may be that more of one
As a generation if you may
Mixed with alcohol-the two may just become joined as one
Into the veins
Subsequently in the blood
Then it hits the brain
And as a synopsis you will feel a vitalizing thud
Alcohol will dull your senses
Which in turn-numbs any pain
Turning supposed mental exhaustion
Occasionally and fervently into an unsurpassed situation of gain
Pour me a drink
One or two for the road
Becoming perplexed yet ordained in the center of cautiousness
Yet with a smile the bartender has just okayed
Exhibited myself now in a buzzed stupor a chivalrous ego enters
That to be frank-the more I see, the more I go
A tire pump concealed under my shirt
I now have a very inflated beneficiary alter ego
My conversations run far from dry-despite a stales voice
With illustrious yet firm stories to tell and somewhat confirm
Even if you are obnoxiously bothered
Hide your dismay-And try not to squirm
Pour the young lady in the pink dress a red wine drink
How to strike a conversation with this affluent dame
Even if I try
The solution if not-may still be not-who is to know
Drink
Drink
If I have much more
The cliff of life is short yet long-heck I am on the brink
I only live a mile away
No need for me to drive
For then intimidation would also own the road
Call a friend
Associates is what my actual term should be
For in this great expanse-At least one must prove their care and share
As I am on this Friday night spree
My mental balance is sequestered
My body appears nearly whole
I do feel somewhat disorganized yet suppressed
I promise to the Almighty
I will carry on decently and wonder now if I am as if them
Protect
Serve
Keep the peace
And help
Sometimes I actually question my own authority
A life of obligation
An unclaimed minority
WRITTEN BY: Brian Moilanen 2013

Pride or Merely Principality

You are a source of self worth and even sometimes conceit
Add the two obdurate charges together
And do you notice the prognostication that leans towards deceit
Where is the cut-off line and which of the two does impose
Look at me-and what I have accomplished
Would it be wrong to either judge or suppose
Look at yourself and the track record left for others to view
Would it be up on library's ledger
And if so-would it remain dormant or be up for review
If someone unknowingly stole a word from the book
Would you forgive or would you aim to sew
Case in point
Move forward moved by principality and not by pride
Jump in the passenger seat of my car
And welcome now to infinity- I will boast-so say hello to the ride
Find the local diner and do not pass off on
A hot cup of black coffee, eggs, bacon and buttered toast
What is the protocol and original draft for a situation of this
Negotiating between pride and power of a jurisdictional prince
Talk of the town
Or is the mind playing tricks
Is it now that you see the mind and soul in balance
The compassion of craftiness lays downs it cards-yet with subtle dispersed hints
I call it- others pride
Others have the grandeur of saying it is principality
Divide the pie into sections or pieces
Look at lives edges
Observe the middle and not obstinate the creases
Is it all privilege
Is this what you would call all a controlled prerogative of probity
So much in this adjourning world
Even the half blind are able sometimes able to completely see
Yet what is it exactly that these often times bickering ones do see
Is it the half clothed human being
Roles of impecunious-Is this the poor mans implication for a jurisdictional plea
Worse yet-tired and alone and just waiting to flea
Something needed-although to govern thee
Is that person of justice-that man of virtual patience going to ever locate me
I think so
But I know myself- greater than thy fellow man
Which brings back to justice
What is the ultimate plan-pride or principality
How much does it take to flip the scale of justice
Or do we need a medium to be congruent and for the future to foresee
When prayers go without answer
Is it that our timetable is not that of our higher powers
For heavens sake-cut the yard
For the limbs are most beautiful sage pleasant flowers
What- ever your decision
Good luck and may God entwine and intervene
Seeing through what is hallow is a gift of certainty displaying the serene

WRITTEN BY: BRIAN MOILANEN 2010

Purgatory-or Mankind Vision of Limbo

End of earthly life
Madness involved in which where a soul does now go
A far cry from fairy tale logic
Where the cupids arrows been launched-and signifies a significant love show
Yet I suppose an ethereal vision
Of other worlds involving romance is another end time mystery
This is not my current exact focus
So lay this all aside-mythical magic is despite my saying-folklore
Much to speak about where an expired time soul does next explore
The agnostic belief is simple...
Birth, life, death, grave
Yet with their idea of focus
Does anyone have a soul at all-anything celestial in which to save
Some Christians for example ….
Believe in the belief of Christ thru God
And that there is already furnished and reserved for every deserving soul
A place within eternity-call it heaven-which most people only dream
Where is then purgatory
Catholics have their own understanding
That the trinity of God is the sole belief
That this God of their following has its own customs
When someone dies
They immediately go to a resting place of the dead
Where they will find out if they have made the grade for heaven
Lives actions and reactions will pass as...as...if a movie of corrected design
If this is based upon Catholic design and not to mention a few other religions
Will you be upright-and walk the line
Walk the earth
That is what the deceased belief to a sort of the Holy bible-being a coded book
Christ will judge not only the soul-yet also the living and the dead
Where they know nothing-see nothing-and are completely dead to the worlds that does surround
Christ shall walk the earth a 2nd time as lore does exhibit from the biblical past
And then your soul will fortify and come to life
As the body and soul-of someone quite alert and awake
Rectification
Sanctification
Rising from the dead
Also I must note and let you know
144,000 souls if you study the good book
Have automatically earned a saved soul
Much of their lives beforehand were written by the owners good choice
Extolled and polled-by God and via Christ
If you are one of those 144,000-live it up comfortably and solemnly rejoice
Once again all in tombs-shall be raised
And those souls currently in heaven
Will await the nu-found souls and be not dazed
Believe
Do what you must
Hold true to religion-talking to Christ
A form of undying goodness with cherished sometimes simplistic trust

WRITTEN BY: BRIAN MOILANEN 2010

Puzzle of Preponderance

I am being surpassed in this lifetime by a monumental weight
Dominated and possibly overtaken by a strange surreal unforeseen force
Is my slate per-written immaturely
And thrown off of its total free willed choice–now being blinding discriminate power
My attempt to cleanse myself of the choices which remain
Yet I have strictly vowed and attempt to never be overly preeminent and cower
Despite what does mentally tarnish and physically stain
Puzzle of preponderance
Can I possibly realistically partake to solve this maddening puzzle
Although I am not a bit parched
Alone and by myself-drink in hand I will vulnerably guzzle
Never did I consider alcohol a friend of mine
Yet this bottle seemingly nurtures so therefore I do nuzzle
I am inside
Such as you are to me-investigating my every move
I feel as though I am at a 70's disco dance party
Yet do I have the touch-do I have the disengaged groove
Is it possible to win the war
Yet haphazardly oddly enough to win the battle
Get the situation- half right at least
Claims the sacramental administrator of my particular religion
Taste the holy wafer of Christ's portrayed body
Communion rebirths itself on this Sunday with just a smidgeon
Privilege-The honor of choice concedes within time
Options
Supposed choices
All lead to always supposedly -ones cup of tea
Do the math-cover the obtuse angles of science and bondage of mankind
And I sure do hope that you feel free
Where has this freewill went
Freewill seems to have destined itself out of my days
Now I have become a search light soul
Searching while confused and not with rose colored glasses- gazing amongst the haze
Is each day a brand new beginning
If so let my prior engagements equaling bondage
Not secure me too tightly
So I do not ever become hostage
Please forgive
Am I still confused
At the table of life I sit and intervene with praying
Yet have been cornered with anxiety and everybody's bill
I just won't quit
Perplexed-yes of course
I would sing a lullaby of fluid joy to your new one
If my voice was not labored with disparity
Or is it insecurity-my voice has become rather hoarse
I still pray for others
Even those forbearing the worst
I have been there before-maybe even today
But I remember I am blessed-not vexed or cursed

WRITTEN BY: BRIAN MOILANEN 2010

Resurrection of the Holy Angel

Powerful and dazzling open eye light
What else currently matters
Except the adoration of love-angel eyed sight
Do your envisioning
Go ahead-watch and securely gather; keep eye on your right
Do not retreat-the chance of a life time is here to cordially use
I swear it somehow
Momentarily these lips can't regale or deception with fraud
To observe an angel
Is to observe an angel
Is utmost praise to the Almighty in proper laud form
Feeling the self exultation and renewed
My spiritual form is beyond pleasant-not at the others present norm
The feelings of intimacy appear to be at an utmost high
Fiesta and love ranges in all direction
Nothing at all to deny
Therefore the need for any misguided detention
I suppose it is time to rise, restore, or simply revise
Resurrection brings you from the dormant of any demise
Fully functional and now without its blemish-purified
Life or this day begins-sanctified and fully equipped and supplied
I have no delight in which denied
Possibly a prophet
Or could I be a new aged saint
So much deity and customary allegiance-all marks of good nature
Please don't allow yourself to deteriorate from within-do not faint
As you know an angel is far superior to man
Yet within the light of the shadows
Just maybe mix in the midst of what is within
A spiritual being that is just also tempted-yet strays from sin
God's holy order of hierarchical beings
Yet without pride or arbitration that compounds offensive man
Man must work extra hard to earn the holy land; his eternal destiny
Because so much of what of these transgressions do not fit in the ultimate plan
That is where an angel lie or lay
Yet just how much benediction does manifestation actually take
Forgive that animal of initial disregard-and comfort the snake
Bored with desire to console
Heck-cook up an angel cake
Speaking of an angel
If you have not seen one yet
I believe in time-that at certain time and place that you will
Mesmerized by action alone
You will partake someday of righteous action and the throne you will help fulfill
Although even with belief and credence
I suspect with even alone these two attributes you are debuted
Comfort of the holy angel
The pond of ever flowing spirits and radiance will have continually spewed

WRITTEN BY: BRIAN MOILANEN

Running Both Hot and Cold

Impeding
Receding
Mentally bleeding
Falsified loss or albeit was it an immense gain
Following rules-To thy own self be true
Perseverance the way in which you stay intact committed to be together
Of these –All form components such as glue
Yet sticky enough to bind up the wispy debri that of a feather
Forgive
Forget
Particularly not engrossed with your own personal choice of religion
Yet silent echoes in my heart find me back at the start-bewildered contentment
Chores and tasks always somehow get done
Do what you must and never disclose God's perfect son
Give praise where praise be inured
Be cautious-as certain hearts maybe very fragile
So they can entertain while endure this land without being injured
Sometimes ice cold; frigid frontier
Coins flip sides
And I place my bets on what occurs often-yet near
Put the two emotional essentials in an electric blender
And out comes a liquid substance that is splendid-a drink ready to be bought
Insight I acquire-Yet I am not a social expert
In actuality understanding my own self-I am at a standstill
Abstention of prejudice and allowing for ethnic discretion I am
Having more than ample wisdom for lives struggles-I cannot ever be portrayed as a sham
A way of rivaling myself and never disregarded as a phony
Seemingly unreal
Interesting to frolic desire and want yet allowing for fabrication of money
Yet doubts internally begin to prefer their manifestation
The enlightenment is the pacifist with cure-similar to zeal
Let us spread this across the desperate nation
Do your own intervention
For once or at a minimum
Be the boss of your own life
Don't allow the dark to chase the shadows
Neglect what appears as ever present strife
And if these plans fall short
Squash up all work –then find the wastebasket and toss
I believe that the x marks the spot
Obviously our intensity does not carry or always run on high
And if in a suppressed mode
Switch to overdrive
And….I bet that you more than likely will
For a race competed in last place
Only brings its passed time-And minimum of thrill

WRITTEN BY: BRIAN MOILANEN 2010

Sarcasm

Judging every movement of prattled and ruffled human thought
Criticism-waging war through volatile verbal warfare
I am able to read between the lines
And with me-see that you do not care
How much of words being truly unkind evidently remain
The enemy is now within the gates-yet how much does that ultimately scare
Persisting and remaining to lie lay low
Is it true I should attempt to carry on my merry way
And turn the tide-or even the tables
And in my small world with this newfound power-declare a holiday
Fight back I must or definitely should
Exposed to danger from uncaring betrayers
Did I in fact make my point-If so- am I understood
Creativity of the soul allocates to chronologically the next step
Harboring an equal mentally ordained fanciful playfield
And if there were a judge
How much of this character assassination would he eventually yield
Derivatively I feel somewhat refined
And other times I understand the wages of symptomatic war
Not with cannon, rifle, or bullet
Yet with word of mouth-Almost somewhat attached to the core
Considered by most to be a sophist
All things usually go with plan and form of rhetoric
So if you think you have blindly mislead me
Check your war plan again-because you cannot petition-you are downright sick
What is the anatomy
Better yet….
Just how is your brutality of breath comprised
I know who and what you are
Therefore your design of delirium has me not surprised
I always do my implications and strategies of homework
And being ahead of this game-it is you who need to revise
Should in return-I also verbally denounce
Because often enough your smiling sarcasm appears to socially-do no wrong
Yet the density attached
Is noticeable and so very pungent-being vainly strong
I will express
I will speak my mind
And in effort-I hope you will confess
Henceforth-I will put the cassette conceding truth back into rewind
Soon I will abundantly scold and in turn-not wither
Yet remember all of my bad days and soon again find
Leave me be
Alone I must on occasion be kept to stay
Along we must all get
And since you are playing this game
Non- compliance is valued-only as a forfeit
I will win through by what I did not ever deserve
Challenge me again
And it is you who then avoids dread and misunderstands nerve

WRITTEN BY: BRIAN MOILANEN 2010

Solutions Versus Problems

Perplexing-all of this with a twist of cards and its bends
Time moves forward and always makes it amends
Slowly
Sometimes quickly-even indifferent
Solving is the issue
And when gone without loved ones too long
It brings about...I miss you
Disciplined action
With uncertain reaction
Is there ever going to be satisfaction
Better respond with although confidently-required time
Deadlines and agendas
Lists, plans, and scheduled times
Possibly infuriating it seems at first
Cure the hunger-obey and abide the corresponding thirst
Problems for everyone-involving course of events that may seem the worst
Welcome to your life
Sickly-other people may feast on the problems of others
Respect does respect itself I suppose
So then-can we not be as if sisters and brothers
Do not be shallow-step up to the plate
And battle the woe
Through it all
Something although and despite-seems unclear
Are the end of these current problems getting near
Or only calculations of adversity-hesitantly adding to fear
Determining just what leads to what is unkind
Heck with rewind-courageously live in the now-forward progress you will find
Heartache and more-are all added determinants of the grind
Have the ability to strive for what others plead for more of
A 6 foot winged holy dove
Yup….the attack of joviality on my behalf
In an electric jungle
Twice as tall as the toughest prey-an 18 foot giraffe
As you can see life is not a vacation
Or neither is it a task
Borrowing from botched plan
I will not walk
I watch as my competition has fled and ran
I will fly
Whether with wings or not
I see only solutions instead of delinquency
I hit the targeted spot
And I see your target all along-was the burdened-yet winning me

WRITTEN BY: BRIAN MOILANEN 2010

Supplied Soul

Space
Surrounds us and is virtually within itself
Universe
Where does it begin-on God's table or his shelf
super-naturalism
What undying force controls it all
Extrasensory perfection
Communication of only the gods or also man too
Divinity
Given by God and allowing devotion as properly what to do
All of this causes internal schism
Refraction of light; refraction of brain causes its own prism
Angels
Superhuman and also winged; super-close to the Almighty
Everything else apparently in between
And even the blind do principally see
All are supplications to the hungry soul
As for spirits
In this game they wander this earth and play their role
Telepathy
Communication without gesture or spoken word
Spirits
A form of messengers-an appearance of is nearly impossible, quite odd
Take a moment to think
Do you or I know more than others`
I am awestruck
What an establishment of loving sisters and brothers
I am awe-struck and on the brink
Slanderous world
Well….not totally
Yet to a degree
Open your eyes to falsehoods
Now….Do you agree
Black and blue
Colored to every shade in-between with hue with tint
Do you see and understand this world demands God
Or should I just stare off into amazement-take a hint
The old fashioned adage still does exist
Good versus bad
Bad versus good
Phonies unfortunately help line this game with discerning info
Those spirited and enlightened with God turn the tables
And help to enlighten this upwards battle
Jump on the horse
That is-If you can locate its saddle

WRITTEN BY: BRIAN MOILANEN

That Conditioned Voice of Thought

Expectations needs expressed with its ongoing figurative want
Inside the mind the processes of complexity diverge
Without hesitation the inkling of perception begins to unfairly taunt
That superior-yet also necessary voice of thought
Sometimes I holler within eternally- so as not to fall apart externally
Keep myself together -in all its facets and other interesting forms
This boarding house of reaction-includes with action-even the good book
The pages do turn delicately slow-as if being read in forums
The significance laid down both in praise and precious word
Walking upright-and not a bundle of nerves-being uptight
To stay mentally clear-and miles from what is deemed to be absurd
The inner voice
Chaotic uprisings-such as the abrupt changing of the seas tide
Keep me posted or in other words-at bay
Include me in the collections of advent-for the sanctimonious ride
Renditions
Maybe so to say-surrendering by way the music of sound
Or-is it the other way around
Surrendering by way the sound of music
Play the chords correct and in tune
And watch the bass chords get an astounding flick
With those strumming fingers
Observe that hand give a slight with the pick
Absorbed with the flooding of the musical pitch
Voices of reality or is it fantasy
Throw its audience in a twitch
Get conditioned with a brain that submits to a calculated change
Or will it merely in time just rearrange
Within accordance to its occupational range
What goes through the mind
Generates its heat-accumulated by a thrust of heart with brain
If this is paralleled as being congruent with force
Do you then feel the strange strain
Conditional
Forms of mind frame that always differ and subsequently tweak
Transitional
Through the conscience itself they shall always speak
We all change-whether we like it or not
Time it waits on nobody
Repairing of all senses unique-the x marks the spot
Talking to a hierarchy of angels
I realize now my voice of reason contained-has also been sealed
Such as the 7 seals that will open someday
The end of it all-will soon be revealed
What is it exactly that you believe
It all depends upon the choice of your voice
And what the irony of the matter always does conceive to receive
Also must I add-what your senses envelope to fathom
Which is indicative merely as what you truly do perceive

WRITTEN BY: BRIAN MOILANEN

That Inner Silent Drama

Inevitably
It will find a way to sneak considerably into your impressionable day
That inner silent drama
Which fashions itself as clueless and barely catchy in every single way
Do you feel free-And is your mind playing tricks
Is it one of those days
Will my broad mindedness be something in which good I may add
Yet situational madness as this is discomforting
Not only for me yet also my enemy who is mad
Drama queens and drama kings
Forthright justice with twisted allegiance
Is this what this life of emotional amplitude brings
Strange events
Collapsing situations
Times that are and seem to be at a world-wide doom
Look behind your back gradually
Actually now looking onward as emotional actions loom
Sink or swim
Walk or run
My perceptions seek courage despite what appears as grim
Does the perfected delectable breakfast
Always go savored down to the last bite
Colossal
Large in speculation of life and the neighboring world
Do you not allow although for these actions to possessively bring you down
Sad on the outside yet smiling within the inner
There goes the marvels of the natural diversified clown
Who by agony alone becomes tired of the discord and disbelief
How is it possible to obtain the glorified crown
When most of all you own is contradicted grief
Is the biggest enemy myself
Concurring with what and what I have not accomplished
Do you also understand my love for my fellow man
Sifting mostly water instead of gold
Benefits the holder and not necessarily the universal saving plan
In this life whom do I serve the most
A feast with God- the speculation of heavenly worth
Who is able to forgive sin and rewrite texts
Even before the thought of one's own birth
I have sinned
It is the nature of an undisciplined soul
Occasionally I feel the blazing fire even while on this planet earth
Vile subordination is able to take its overwhelming toll
Do your best
Stay on track
Tame your inner demons
A soft spoken man's word-which I hope penetrates and does not lack

WRITTEN BY: BRIAN MOILANEN

The Distance Between Us - U.F.O's

Off in the distance
Just exactly is it that these eyes do see
An illusion
A distorted glow of lights and such
So close yet to be exact- so far
A flotsam on the windy rigid wet sea
At its accord yet it compels such as angry war
A suppressed and mind with blood flow transfusion
Something being snatched and detached
I this a neurosis or ….what is it
A twisted reverse of brain order-an illusion
The colors
Difficult to detect the separation of
A hurried feeling that is disenchanting
And appears to be void of even temporal love
As mentioned-I am not at all mentally off
Even although
My brain with mind it does mentally scoff
A dogs howling yelp
A strong wind in the breeze
At once-I feel hopeless
And plead for help as I cower upon my knees
Off to the immediate East
Call it 8 'o clock as if in military fashion
I realize what either believers or skeptics fathom
And for thee first time observe what fuels their passion
I am now fully aware and mobile once again to witness
What is definitely an unidentified flying object
I can see it
I readily feel the radical change of events
No longer am I although besieged with terror
Interest invades me downright to the soul
An occasion such as this-nothing could be rarer
A star-ship
Or possibly to my belief- a light phenomena
Yet I am extraordinarily assured
From this day forth flashbacks only now amount to insomnia
The next day as I returned
From the short one mile walk
I read the papers and over 47 separate
Accounts of these spectacular sightings
My finger-nails appear jagged as they are able
Notice all the force of habitual swayed tidings
Wow….
What to say and much beyond that what now to do
Life a problem with hidden solution game
And I hope to hold the ratchet with the screw
Turn the ratchet
In hopes of a fix
Are you a believer
The upside obtained by Christ on the crucifix
Bi-God
Was I nearly abducted by alien classification
It was though observing an electronic Frisbee

89

Ordained with lights yet sustained by about 100 times or so the size
I speak no lies-take this as valid truth
That night left me to only calculate and revise
Aliens
Or are they cyborgs of space
What is their purpose
What are they about
A million times a million planets-maybe more
Galaxies and vast ends of light years accompany black holes
Maybe there is intelligent life
That has beyond satisfaction in store
Study past findings and stories of
And let your mind work with-let it explore

WRITTEN BY: BRIAN MOILANEN 2010

The End of It All

Absolutely nothing left
Eyes witness nighttime's dark that no longer abounds
Therefore oddly also no lite
Beyond that an untimely end shadowing all earthly sounds
Without fight
Without flight
Creatures of all kind drop out of sight
A galaxy of 100,000 galaxies
Also see a complete sudden tragic end
I beg my dear Lord for reconciliation in which to mend
Yet after all-just what is left to send
An enormous void captures a chilled iced earth
Where lite rays won't prism or even bend
Now going without common factors such as principle
Nearly nothing left with exactly zero to lend
A chronicling brain-not sure of the year
Albeit-not really quite sure of the time
Ultimately despite I know that angels are near
To finish cordially in the Almighty's final rhyme
Saving souls and wiping away any tear
God Almighty to intervene and give hope
Heavenly euphoria grasps at when the tomorrow will near

WRITTEN BY: Brian Moilanen 2013

The Essence of Yesterday

The tie that binds
Complying with virtue
Watch as the time on the clock just rewinds
Yesterday
Yes I feel it in my hands and heart
How can we see the ending
If we don't notice any start
Christ centered
Coming smack dab to middle ground
Dignity often times works with miracles
And evidently once again is found
The essence of yesterday
The soft tone on the radio playing is
Lacking any flavor yet still is sweet
Welcoming a day in which to reminisce
A lovers touch
Catered with a tranquil sweet kiss
Adhering to the good times
Those certain moments that we always will miss
Reading also a letter of old
My heart bleeds and longs for the past
I react upon my environment of images
And upon the stage am part of the cast
Back through time that of about 20 years
Many good times
Which coincide with also the sad
Obtaining recollections fruitfully
A way in which to tame those that were mad
We watch the children pray
Save us God today
Come whatever may
Without any word spoken
I still understand what you didn't say

WRITTEN BY: Brian Moilanen 2013

The Unknown–Day of Reckoning

End of calendars
End of years-henceforth this is the end of days
Minutes appear ensconced-and now wind down
The world is abruptly being enrolled and has
No tomorrow and actually nothing much more left
Envisioning either the beginning of the day of atonement
Or if 4 leaf clovers will blossom and we are still to be fortunate
Not much more than the breaking and busting of one of the seals
This is a duty and privilege of mine-which I hold and manifest
Oceans waters are not challenged as of yet-still colored teal-another final test
God must reign until he hath put all enemies under his feet
Is it possible to convert one million agnostics along with their non believers
Will God please hear me-as I with game plan-have openly confessed
Or is it truly worldly-too late
God will violently avenge-and weeks prior
Shall with destruction contained wrath-completely demonstrate
It is not only Israel cut off from the true Messiah
But surprisingly the entire world has lost all special favor
The grand finale is beginning to advent
With what I only assume-tear drops to savor
The day of the Lord
What if my hands are those
That hold that mighty Godly sword
I must keep up with these biblical teachings as keynote
Of God's holy-fair-just and kind most respectable Holy Word
For our knowledge-The Almighty has more names
More names than just….King of kings and Lord of lords
Also 16 other Old testament names-even names such as….Shalom
Which means-The Lord is my peace
The church before has been my refuge and home
And by sentiment it is my faith through release
Back to the subject at hand
Will on this day the 1rst seal be opened and the final battle begin
Or merely the 7th seal be opened and worked from within
Through sentiment near in the future-There will be one final shocking revelation
The sanctification
Explaining a vindication
That supremely Jehovah is ruler of this creation
And that his obedient tried son Jesus-is ruler over all creation
And that beside Israel Christianity is practiced throughout every nation
This is my true remedying proclamation
That releases its own type of supplementation
Times on this earth get tough-as nails
Yet never as wicked-as the horrors of hell
Remember this before you sleep
And to that-even before you awake
For God does allow-thought attached to destiny
For God does not exist in that permanent penalty those being the fiery lake
Observe the almighty angel-before I am forgotten
Remember that ordained holy apple from Genesis
For through it all-it had never became rancid or rotten

WRITTEN BY: BRIAN MOILANEN 2013

The Ups and Downs of Diversity

An instance or a point of difference with
The condition of being different
We are not at all the same-or are we
If so-have you seen my identical down to the clad, me
A clone so to speak
An exact match-one of the same
If you have measured up to these findings
Then tell me-would you denounce or praise-this being a valid claim
Hitch-hiking
Mountain-biking
Brain-psyching
To a point-we all practice maybe not another form of way or hist
Possibly fathomless madness
Obliging to this endeavor I earn possession that is unable to resist
The ups and down of diversity
Is it flipside up....
And downside-merely just suitably down or radically low
Now to get cantankerous and with hiatus
Where to search for religion-and with which theater plays quality show
Everyone....obviously everyone-has features that represent them as unique
Having talents and yet unique
O?
Now on the other hand- some have quirks and oddities of nil
If that is your picture-than by all means-get prescribed a remedy pill to embellish within
Although this does not necessarily market insanity
And for the matter....not even necessarily sin
Do I need group therapy
Guided and with demonstrations by counselor and peer
I have been there before.,
Instead of help-all my love of life seemed more near
Abolished
Demised
Can I not self do it myself-have It all revised
Strange days
Occurring ways
A thickened haze
Comforting dramatic plays
Subdivide
Feelings that usually divide
Enjoy your sports car ride
Add it all up
Still a dollar short
Report to your maker-if you choose
That
That within your soul and brain
Problems and solutions do contort
Drink a glass of red wine at the resort
Export
Purchase from your neighbor in length and distance
Break the mold
Search for a queen-as you are that prince

WRITTEN BY: BRIAN MOILANEN 2010

The Way I Feel

Bestowed
A way to get rest responding in tranquil
Is to know-as with the majority few-I am determined and significantly owed
Skeletons in the closet
Slightly off the straight edge-just by a near cut
Ostracized-calculated war by an opponent of hypocrisy
Yet-do not have faith in yourself and maddening propriety
For this dazed frenzy I am in-is mediocrity
I do not necessarily agree with these contradictions
Appearance of being disturbing-yet invoking thought indeed
Incurring to or without ego and mental inflictions
May seem actually more or less as derelictions
Shake hands with the unknown-charted as possibly more
A way to understand the battle
And securely learn why there is any need at all for war
Superstitions
Magic held in belief with required twist of law to nature
Apparitions
A tell tale piece remains of ghostly occurrence
Endurance
Also like dominoes that collide and fall-will have their recurrence
How awing to visibly notice or see their outward appearance
The way I feel
What I study-doctrines of discipline of calling of duty
A blemish with chemistry available-a plan chained by utter conceal
My brain responds with disinclined choice yet it is subsided
Yet as for my body-it is complete yet transported in total appearance
Anytime-anyplace
You and I equal to the premise of involvement
What is my covert secret catch phrase
To pacify our inward resolving and involvement
Become humble quickly and thread nimble all my days
Not try to dig
Or for that matter with my own force-by hand
Pull a 30 thousand-pound rig
Going neither where I need not belong
A new modern day psalm of humanism
Is totally shy when it comes to schism
Wildly my brain may run a bit wild
Yet dislike-produces tragic error
Topic of soft-yet subtle
Should although never demise-within its own terror
Forward-on the spot
Speaking elusive chain of event
If you do not understand this dark prophet
It is now up to you-reconcile-gather and continue to repent
Be considerate to your maker for all the days that he has plentifully lent
As in baseball-find home plate
And step up-ready for the pitch
Hold on tightly to the word in which I speak
And scratch that inner driving recurring itch
WRITTEN BY: BRIAN MOILANEN

These Goods Are Not Damaged

Undoubtedly-you have seen me before
Trace through your own records and books of merit
So therefore do not allow for violating maiming neglect
Obviously you assimilate through actions of your own worth
Yet abilities reprogram regimen and gather to redirect
What I bring is anything composed of virtuous good
Possibly it is you that doesn't understand my consigned afflicted condition
Or uniquely and imposingly enough
Is it profoundly misunderstood or barraged
That slightly enough the one mildly vexed might actually be you
Mental issues
Paradox-are you into the realms of the mentally unknown
Hear what I say and my valiant attempts to disregard opposition-only to succeed
Admonitions with words of clever come from me via the telephone
It was a pleasure to have heard from you
Deal with me If I am slightly off
I reach for the skies only to grab a star
So do not incorrectly jeer or rudely scoff
I carry my weight as a salesman
Hereafter I put on a circus like show to push off my goods
And soon if I do not get a purchasing buyer or buyers
I could figuratively get lost in the thick heartless woods
My goods though are not damaged
At a miniscule there might be a speck of rust
Yet they are genuine and of exceptional worth
And contain with each a statistic of security and trust
Yet now your mind may wander with and you will ask yourself
If legitimate products were not ever sold
Then even the non perishable would somehow suffer
And even wood and plastic would become as mold
Now here comes a situation of where stands your soul
Coming clean
Totally serene
Don't drive sporadic-watch for that middle-lane ravine
Bad feelings dislodged and emotions that seem irate and mean
Kind of obscene
Count your blessings to reduce the dormant sorrow
If you can keep yourself together
More sun than rain will explore your bright tomorrow
A world wrought by God hand is primarily with light
Consider your problems small to minimize others sufferings
And not stress up on what keeps us all a little uptight
Follow the center
To stay from the dark corners that could suck you in
Providing this theme of central aversion is attained
And all sane views to say the least is which in what I mean
Do not label or make assumption of fellow soul
If so in doing
Your square dice wont turn instead they will rock and roll
Keep the faith
For it won't hurt one bit
If the shoe is the right size
The course of action directs it to commonly fit
A fit into a modified yet crazy world
A shape into a sale
Now when you speak heads will turn and be assured
If they do not firmly listen
They are at a loss-As prime opportunity became blurred
What am I creating in concoction for antidote
And fortunately enough the attackers were those that stirred
WRITTEN BY: BRIAN MOILANEN

Things Left Unsaid

What should have been modestly said-at a minimum per say
Has passed my voice again for this moment
On we go-with another passing day
The radio that is on comforts these empty spaces once again
The I love you's
Those fleeting moments that eventually just drag on past
What if yesterday was your first chance
And now going unsaid-today were you and your quieted dispositions last
Those people in your life whom you love and care for
Take a 2nd chance just to say that you regard to them with joy
Time may pass quickly
Yet even that moment gratifies as if-a treat to a puppy or even a new toy
The mind plays part of the medium
While the soul dictates between brain and heart
Years pass quickly
And life is now-the entity-or ourselves we can never freshly restart
So live in the today
Try to get on past all those yesterdays-for they do pass ever fast
Some-days seem huge compared to others
Colossal-yet hurried-somewhat vast
The simplicity of a dollar card itself
Is able to say more than the words thus it does bring
A picture of a loved one attached emancipates
The souls heart to rectify and also to pleasantly sing
Things although left unsaid
In accordance therefore has nothing in which to cling
When to speak
Whom to confide in
And which way to know what merits a new friend-possibly to applause
All the mental cuts of misfortunes that have by accident nearly fled
I honestly wish I had a roll of invisible gauze
To heal
To conceal
Possibly even to unveil
Yet what of the future-what would it reveal
Or against the grain of hope-would my word be utterly stole
I suppose that I although if ransomed-could pay the toll
As my plate consistent of a feast-would be eaten
And I would be surprised-not demised-and pleasantly full
What about others
I care often for those who I do not even know
Compassion at its finest
For poverty knows everyone-who has or is faltered-and on skid row
I speak to God
And yes….He does listen
Like a Christmas adorned with lights and metallic strings
How beautiful it does vibrantly glisten
Angels
God's messengers
Ministering spirits of salvation
Celestial
Cover-yet with tremendous voice-this whole complete creation
Have a nice day
And at least for sanity's sake

Learn how to give-whatever the situation
And as for this story- it shall give as it also does take
Do not forsake
O.K.
From time to time it may allow its path to permit
Yet if burdened
Allow for passage-and for heartache to surrender and quit
Care-Concern
Both equal to itself-as a way to love thru learn
I shall say no more
As my head full of question-begins to continue to churn
I feel the need to retire
As a new day draws near-and I watch as the time does steadily just burn
WRITTEN BY: BRIAN MOILANEN

Triumphs or Tragedies

Is this nu-found effort that you pleasantly came across
What most would define as a major victory
Or just another form of drama that substantiates as a loss
If we serve a just and pure creator that employs goodness
How could I argue-that this splendid entity is also my boss
Nestled within a profusion of totally different extremes
A hint of light pervades and a sunshine seemingly beams
Who owns my heart and soul-I become regarded by a boss that shares
A new day interestingly enough I do greet
Acceptance of what divine reality really is
Trying my hardest to avoid bitterness and defeat
An added pleasure anoints me
And yes I do uniquely and cautiously compete
Adding names to the Lambs book of life
For those who possibly believe in authenticity of John 3:16
Do you see what I say
And precisely just what I mean
Self righteous I am not
Observe God's holy word
As an effort to be contained-and also successfully taught
Maybe I am back to square one
Acceptance and denial both relentlessly compete
As a distressed nagging cry that of a goat
Can somebody please lower the volume of this cantankerous bleat
Also to change subject at hand
This street of slippery concrete
Forward I drive and am in command
I must realize-if you have your health and a relationship with Christ
Everyday is a gift and smile as you are truly alive
Mental and brain induced diaries we all do own
The Almighty moves quickly in my life
Consecrated quality-I do await the day to sit at his throne
Will I pass
Or fail in tried solemn regard
Playing lives poker
As I pray for sanctimonious effort- I throw down this last card
Written By: Brian Moilanen 2103

Twice the Man

A gallon or so of fatal fluid-call it an arsenic chemical death
Is only abolished with an ounce of love and antidotes cure
Welcome immediately now to a heavenly devotion
With the nearing majority-we are now on lives purpose-and we do tour
Awakening occasionally yet-not all the documented time
-With earnest desire I have stepped to the anticipated plate
silence and modify those weak in mind and spirit
And with my home run-salvation is never too old or nearing being late
If you want to be a devoted follower of God
Then….well….just say it
Twice the man requires advanced arbitration from soul to heart
You-such as me-understand these sort of revelations of covert secrets in which to cling
Jesus through God understands all of these tribulations
And destined prior to it even happening-we hear the flock of testy pigeons sing
Life is not amassed by what we own
As for the joneses-life is only about what we have-life is so to say….a thing
But yes
The heavy side is able to demonstrate nearly the loss of love and unconditional feeling
Even if harbored in a hospital bed in desperate critical health void of feeling
Although flawed-you eventually will generate sight for the importance of God through stable life
May time pass quick-As there is much more than you know-than to just look gloomy into a ceiling
Mania and mental condition-I understand your consorted odd excitability
The biblical number of more than just one
Actually might be resorted to the number three
The three wise men never ever gave up upon the Christ child
And yes they also went amongst trials-when passed it is another case of being free
Which consolidates to the proclamation of nothing more….
Than just leave me be
Live your life
And therefore I will lead mine
A glass of vintage red wine that is high spirited
Yes I do today feel fine
Shrouded in mystery to a degree
Those who walk with Christ
Want to-yet it is often mirrored image or less image of what they see
Themselves portrayed through others
A way in which God and spirits talk and speak
Listen to your calling
And even by telephone the electronics may properly tweak
That is if you are truly wanting
And it is the others that manifest the absence of God- eternally they do wreak
Remember also that no one is sexually immortal
The bible notes henceforth in full reference and maintenance about
If you lead a life of only sin
Rethink-And understand that even prayer alone is a way out
Of prison-maybe strangely if it is only in mentality
Speak your mind
And reason with thee

WRITTEN BY: BRIAN MOILANEN-2010

Understanding Emotions of Everything

Am I as changeable and also as well as impressionable
I feel as if I am lacking due to other individuals infamies
Yes-my existence through faith or fact is impressionable
How to keep a mouth shut forever
Much of my life has its preponderances and is all completely mentionable
Exploitations
Make it all-not just some of-well known
The hush –hush and hocus pocus
Gathers and is centered upon the telephone
I hear your disjointed wave of conversation
And it is exhibited in an odd yet upshot form of vocal tone
What is it that you love-truly
What is it that you hate-Is is something not understood by some
Yet others see it ever-clear and quite newly
Am I off base
Am I able to alter-to help and aide in the process of a mental erase
Common-place
Eradicate the chase
Ethereal visions of other planets
Or maybe also to say-the upper regions of space
Keep on running-with chin up
And only yourself is able to keep the departure of pace
Much of life
Despite what scholars may or may not admit
Is the relation for human contact of a love/hate situation
And there is more than that to even awe-inspiring-even admit
So be bold….where is the humanly proclamation
If not enough is said it can equal mentally to devastation
Be real some will say when apparently-they are way to shallow….
To be real
You need not necessarily to within engage
Yet take it from me
Patterns of misplaced judgments allow enough lecture for anticipated rage
So let us not precede anymore
Yet an antagonist knows despite their illogical reason or surprise
That truth comes with reason
And for those wicked of heart-I promise they will be squashed within the demise
They must understand
Emotions of both the poor and rich somewhat the same
Some want sheer fame
Some-something tangible claim
And others fight off their inner demons
Something in which to tame
Yet to know someone
You must not be to quick to judge
For example-if you judge me-fixated
I just will not budge
Take some time to admire God's green and most set on shore-
Marvelous creation
Even a way to save a buck
Walk with the Lord
And wrath could speak as your sworn enemies-have no further biased luck

WRITTEN BY: BRIAN MOILANEN

Unfailing Ability

Hopefully this burden was successfully lifted off my chest
Yet as though decadently surrounded within myself only now
I feel and wish even my enemies all the best
You have an unfailing ability to know my needs
Henceforth you also understand my wants
Frequent memories and revelations have found me at a young age as before
Baptized in sacred holy water tubs -what is known as the fonts
The small things in life which I seem to adore
I readily fondle while caressing these tender times
Which in token-leaves a carousal and much to explore
My calm yet hungry soul was meant to implore
Impetuously I now feel a sudden physical thrust
Divisions or is it just inspirations from an Almighty God
Opportune while being complete I see it is more than I that I must trust
You give to me
You never impose yourself or strict commands
I am the one desiring and wanting without credible kind host
The unknown soldier
Who is desolate, broken and alone yet still guards his nearly militant post
Do you not understand a good partner is painstaking difficult to find
Review and retrace those precious good memories
So to say-put them all back in the form of rewind
I appreciate
All those goods plus even the material you have given
And they never seem to depreciate
Am I the judge without jury consisting the life of my gift
Be honest-do I ever seem to only officiate
And allow for frugality and accept the term labeled thrift
Now does that make the mark for being swift
The credit card I drop and the cold cash to spend is almost snipped
You are always there for me
Beit emotionally, spiritually, financially and also when in dire need
I thank you with praise and attached is the admiration label
Does this poem make sense
Or is it compared to that more of a fable
Shyness of wording can lead to transparency of reviewed thought
More than the average man
It was just my lives given hand-all the battles I have fought
Yet I thank my higher power
Whom I title as God Almighty
Who gives so much
Medically and sexually-proves me to see
Does your ability ever fail
Have I been kicked off the plains
Without water and feed
You may have just nearly eliminated the Taurus
Yet a master plan still is defiant and abolishes evil in the end
When flat busted and broke
For the homeless man of poverty could a dollar you please lend

WRITTEN BY: BRIAN MOILANEN

Vantage Point or Varlet of Variance

Do you now considerably notice
That fortunately you may have acquired the upper hand
Time goes with and amongst the hourglass
You wide eyed grin-time on your side-as in seeps the sand
Yet a figment of wild imagination-acting as electricity
Quickly runs its hot drifting path-like electricity-with total demand
Who controls the majority of my issues
And is it I-who sustains in variance- in hope of command
But electricity as hot as it transpires-appears hotter that hell
Being shocked more than once-deafens all of your senses
Ears will open in an awestruck type pattern-with many a story to tell
Varlet-menial-some call this average and to the statistical norm
With sincere auditory leanings
From anywhere and at any distance-you are able to detect the storm
Crash of the lightning
Darkening of the sky
Maybe you should run for stable cover
Because this oncoming pain resembles a sigh-or even a resounding silent cry
Exactly where do you measure up in this spectacle of situation
Look to Christ and readily observe
Upon the earth-he was far from being a rich in wealth tyrant
He acquired and gained his power and praise thru an untimely-yet settled nerve
Yet with time-and despite all of this
He-along with Father God's shepherds-lets all on occasion-allow the light-and us to see
Maybe a lot
For others-just a little
I won't die born
As my hands mesmerize the adorned fiddle
Music to my ears
Possibly just harmonic triumphant noise-intrigued by others
Do not ever forget
To this fact-even your most unfortunate brothers
Sisters-they also need and attend to a guiding hand
A life misunderstood
Should never end up being trash-canned
Watch-listen
See-witness
I pray that the spectacle of your lives long days
Are filled with verses-or measures-contained with bliss
Keep in mind others
If so inclined-pray for thy own self
Maybe the latter statement is prodigy's rule
For how many days of life-are included within your own shelf

WRITTEN BY: BRIAN MOILANEN 2010

103

Victim of Design

Hard to say-people are playing games in this field of life
When your number has already been dug before this all began
And more times than not-all you see is the menaced vision of others strife
I can do all things through Christ, because he gives me strength
Yes that is true-Yet he did not mention at what interval and to what appears an endless length
Forever moving towards the heavens I decline in the action of sin
Yet so many closed doors trying for salvation-I see a pattern on how it will be tough to win
I did not intend ever to blasphemes yet am I doing it now
This holy bible is a coded book-and as for a winning game plan
Am I not still wondering just how
How to win
How to avoid over speculation when I am clean
Do you see me challenging bondage
Is somebody out there who understands exactly what I mean
Faith is often the child of fear
All the wreckage upon these bones and battered brain
Christ like I am so to me these words draw near
Is faith born out of calculations in this game of life that we all play
The more I think and emancipate my future
The broader the spectrum-the interest of winning declined by disarray
I am far from being a wimp-yet am growing tired of the born maddening dejection
Look deep into these eyes
And notice the detection
If I were running for the worlds most versatile poet-
Now that would give me hope-as if in an election
Life or should I say humanly existence
Some say is completely cut out or created before our birth
Where is the plotting maze took to next
Inherited battles or a baby with cute colored toy that rattles
I hope freewill has a chance
And to add to that an unlimited speech
If so I am moving closer to God
And Christ the ultimate follower is still within reach
I must continue to pray and adhere to the policies of fortune
Am I going to abode in the heavens
And collect change in my bucket of chagrin
I am able to not transgress currently
And all I see strangely enough is a lucky win
Add up your dollars
Count the change and bless if always-if not at least for now
See life and everything within
As a grazing cow
And allow God to manifest you as a win
A win
A loss
What does incur to what standard
A tie possibly
The more options that you provide through others
Ordained and confident-now you can with the heavens see

WRITTEN BY: BRIAN MOILANEN 2010

War and Peace…. Soon a Release

We will get the best of you if victimized
Ambush your shielding while protecting troops
Until you see-you will be the one targeted while surprised
This is my final testimony-consider this as an enemies alimony
To what extent does this painted black day go
Seaward water moving downstream yet sketchy against the undertow
Plans and planned for checkmate of an attack
If this were chess-it would be bloodied
Opponent the running quarterback-get ready for an all out sack
Dirty, hurt and now all newly muddied
Not a situation of a devil's push
Or that of an angel's lack
Man to man combat crusading
Combat boots on-in the enemies swamp I am waiting
Rifle in hands
Science and strategy applied action seeks reaction
I am trained to battles hilt
And won't be off by even slight fraction
Skill I attain and am focused and had thrilled
Line up those bastards as a stratification
What is the count that I will have to counter- offensively have killed
On the warpath
These attackers will soon see their dictum ….
A bloodbath
We wanted peace
You needed war
Pass the buck to congress
And let us see what the President has in order
The secretary of state panics
And runs down white house covert corridors
Country versus country
No allies-No others want to affiliate
Yet don't press the panic button
For its unveiling power is only mass destruction
More than just a country's demise
And forfeits neighboring allies plus all weapons and supplies
Keep in mind
That we are in the early stage
And yes-peace has its protesting wage
The gung-ho launch -need to encourage weapon of mass destruction
Hatred it made and produced for these certain soldiers
And creates a full body of tormented corruption
Now more than ever we need
A master of peace to establish serenity
And a change of course accord
Not a hush-hush topic
The solver should win the perfect reward
The U.S.
Superheroes known by most
They never go down easy
For we aren't displayed as toast
God save this planet
From all of their convincing demolition
Angels on high are called and active

Soldiers stand fast
God willing-peace begins now
And the believers of unsung victory perplexed say…..
Wow
Give peace a chance and an honorable mention
Chaos is the verdict
Of much of this perplexing hostile tension
God will decide in time alone
If we should wait in anticipation
To give birth to these now faltering and hit –hard nations
Give this a chance
Quiet the evil that has and did surmount-too such high escalated degree
For silencing the dragon-is the new public notice mission for me

WRITTEN BY: BRIAN MOILANEN

War Card

Who has ultimately won
When all have faltered and lost
Except for the machines
Although soldiers throw nearly detonated grenades
And lay waiting ambush within mud huts and grassy ravines
The ultimatum revealed
A cataclysmic battle of man versus cyborg life
Deathly combat of reprisal nearing
Which is recorded as strife-and equaled as war
I myself am confused within this wagered tenacity
And readily count all ammunition
That was allocated within the seething P.X. Store
Wow...A no man's land-that is eerie and quite superstitious
Yet as for my M.R.E. It only keeps me surviving
And is not as Grandmas best-healthy with complete nutrition
Back to the inquired subject at hand
Looking directly at this card of human poker
Realism is poignant-follow military's command
Human soldiers of a million plus ready
Yet to my account-it seems as only a few
Survival of the conscious-as all now are slightly in-betweens
Legitimacy of this Armageddon is polished and focused
And not entitled to be fought with the likes of teens
Decrees of this nature lends as a permanent means
0 horseplay within those moody latrines
We know that you know-human nature is temporarily set aside
War planes glide and surface the mountains summit
Where to run-catch a northbound bus to Canada being the best ride
Bombs fall and gas vapors fill the air-my life falls into depths that plummet
Will you survive to live to see another day
War destroys more than you will ever know
Am I Hollywood-who needs to know
Movie stars film and are on the go
To be continued
To be continued

WRITTEN BY: Brian Moilanen 2013

What Sets You Off

Anger-with it's shake and twist of….
Frustration
Defeated sense of mind with its grains of failure also
Penetration
The bomb seeks a location
On what to hit-why-and how far need be to go
Simply-I am loosing my cool lately
This morning I not only broke-yet stubbed my toe
What sets you off
Truly
What gets your goat-or better yet what is your pet peeve
In a 24 hour day-even without mistake of large
Exit signs find the eyes-as you just want to leave
How much more in which to believe
When glory turns its duplicitous back on you
And discomforts canvassed madness-which opportunely does not relieve
Painting pictures with visions of gold in mind
Yet the future payoff is a ransom of pennies
That was managed to long-suffering find
Brilliant is the work
So brilliant it manufactures a bomb in my head
A mind that is already been at war
A necessary or unnecessary commodity being
That it is difficult to see the sea from the distant shore
The wick is now lit and burning
Beware-and run from me
My heart beats unsteadily
A necessary or unfulfilled commodity
Is danger sometimes
And others-a pleasant surprise-for the poverty stricken to eloquently see
And other times welcomed as
The wick is now lit
Beware-and beware of my bite
Be quick or be dead
Furnished with a pistol
That pumps out the real deal-known as lead
Quieted repressed-furious temperament
Is not alleviated so metaphorically or easily
I am on the courts team of justice
So than what would be the explainable sane plea
Observing a man cheated
Kicked out of his own life
All of these crude elements define leading to rage-which expands to carnage
And not even enough for that much-this is monumental strife
A job applied for once again
A girl asked out accompanied with a box of candy and smiling grin
A letter sent to a loved one-demised by being ripped up
All of these attempts have failed miserably
Failures
The train does derail
Only God now can create sanctimony-with this innocent one
Mental bail
My face turns cold and pale
My blood runs cold

Even being oddly enough-still young at heart
Despite my body withering-I now feel mostly together old
I have been set off
The wick has expired as it once did burn
The bomb only although found in my head
The days from here on better drastically improve
Or I will be another obituary statistic-pages and pages of those diseased-dead
Physically I did not mean too touch you
Or let truth be truth-and show as grim
Yet today is a day where animosity got me
And I am unstable due to the town's predication of my fate
I tried too hard and fastidious
Now what I almost obtained-I miss
Maybe true success was never meant to be
Only monotony-it has always been the plot for me

WRITTEN BY: BRIAN MOILANEN

When I Will Be Gone Forever

Indescribable
Contents that are such as this
Appear long and winding down-nearly insurmountable
Do not confute
Just reimburse and commute
Please-no arguments at this given time
What comes around goes around-only within me you might dispute
Privileges-awards given upon benefit granted and to be enjoyed
You concluded I was not worthy-somehow deemed wrong I became
Which what comes from the inward psyche-the numbers tally-I am annoyed
When I am gone
I will be gone forever
All of this wasted time-I am welcomed to the never
Yet my actions will be continued
Do not mind it being a new home-a new town-a new place
I anxiously await to definitely renewed
Stuck in a situation that comforts more
I would define this as being….glued
I need a taste of spice and speckle of salt
Going day to day seemingly aimlessly
I will be gone soon-you can add me up as gone-the final result
Others say I need to surrender-to your love
Yet there is none-none at all
Two-living under the same roof
I feel as if crumbling-and intimately aloof
With my life
People suggest
Into situations I need not want to be
They subject
Because you cannot pull a living man from the dead
In which with me-you cannot promote to resurrect
Analyze my life
And let me….yes me suggest
Ghost town blues
I would not worry-all that pseudo falseness
Nobody-is advanced enough to give even a truce
Where should I go
I am now estimating-yet not geographically in tune
It is April now
Yet my escape is not on schedule until June
I promise that….
I will disappear
Gone before your eyes even blink twice
We do not see eye to eye
Do you-or I-not fully understand
I am a visionary who is correct
And will follow Christ further-and am in command
We do not read from the same book
Or the same page-In silence
I will attempt and concede at fulfilling my silent inner rage

WRITTEN BY: BRIAN MOILANEN 2010

Which Way Is Up

Which way is up
That dispatches itself and responds-to which way is down
Utter importance concerning both issues-and yet of their subjects
What does up contain-and cleverly reveal
Under-rated nowadays and sometimes forgotten almost
The truth with its attachments-yet perfection cannot be grown or even be remotely real
Real to some
Yet still it backslides and has its imperfections-which is not truly real
So much sin and bondage
The discourse of this action in itself is surely enough-I can effortlessly feel
Promote unfound eagerness with all mirth desire
Zeal now is unshakable and promises much
The unforeseen wick is lit yet responds conclusively-which emits a timid fire
Yet all of this action of cruel corrupt deed ends quickly
As it's shortened pathway does tire
How to get to what is up-and better yet just how far
Focus on religion or even God himself to answer that endearing question
And see not yourself yet precepts of even credos or Eros as that faraway star
Many of times I thought deeply of always going so to say-up
Yet I became overly enlightened
As mere celestial wine overflowed from my Challis gold cup
I became numb
I felt my life indefinite and ordained-yet lacking in scripture-as dumb
Unfortunate with financial reason-As daily bread included with crumb
Those crumbs represent the needy
Sometimes even the desolate
The poor
Yet a good life ahead of them—in store and obviously waiting
Contemplating
When the best time to reward that soul would be
Gee
I suppose and understand in the merits of following-next is me
Yet prayers are always heard from a soul that is sincere
When are those realistic prayers answered although
Stay tuned to the television skies-for the answer is not far-closer than near
I have heard that Christ sanctifies his prayers by the multitudes
And sometimes a prayer that goes unanswered and speaks to others-
Rather than the individual praying him or herself
Is and can be the best prayer yet
That much I put on a gentleman's bet
Although I have had a hard life
I will not regret
Occasionally get upset
Find a solution
To get out of my fret
Because I will-I shall succeed on my lives course and allow its everything-in the middle
Play harmonious rhymes with a fiddle
And let that music bellow-where it must
Up-because now I know that direction
It relies on instinct as its positive thought
Another battle fought
Staying in Gods funded school-which has prevalently taught

WRITTEN BY: BRIAN MOILANEN 2010

Who Am I?

Refreshing news
Appealing such as an unchained gospel
Do angels on high make these auspicious reviews
Speaking not in tongue-yet with fluid dimension
Do you vividly retain what you hear
For what also is seen all adds up to the retention
A neutral suspension
Add it all up and do your own account of the mathematics
Have your ever fallen into a self -fulfilled –is it apprehension
Moreover than that
Am I climbing as high as the galaxy does allow
Sacred wisdom acts as a proposal towards
Not letting big production bring you down-do not have a cow
Not allowing for myself to shudder
Even In the frigid dead of the cold
Fit into this cookie cutting mold
Like a puzzle piece supposedly apt into this game of life
Patiently squashing any competition
No need for weapons-not even a pocket- knife
Laboring against this marvel would make zero for sense
I my competitions head weak or merely slow witted
The synopsis of what I demesne is forward-why be so dense
Stolidity
Stupid and of an unused tarnished brain
I see the comfort of my madness
And feel as though without restrain
I see the restaurant phone
That my dark skinned brother is ciphering and using
He lays out his cards of peace-such as I
Cologne
Watching a world that needs a vigilante chaperone
A brother of peace marginally although does play the spades
The multiply colored water flows sown the structured suite
An alias of charades has him top notch grades
A black and white team entwined with pearl and coal
Furrowed and dented
We both have stories of good guy versus bad guy fights
Now we both disprove
And same mind almost shared understand our citizenly rights
Deny
Reply
Is it true a lie gets trapped within a sigh
Where he just walks away
And smugly gives no way to lightening peace or to pacify
Not king of the jungle
Trapped somewhere amongst the rest in the heap
I hear the rains light tapping
And thru my eyes it begins to seep

WRITTEN BY: BRIAN MOILANEN 2010

Wispy Winding Roads

Winding roads
Turns-twists-and exhilaration with its bends
Ousting outlandish from within this cantankerous mind
All of which mysteriously is emanating and also never-ends
With me I have a lengthy composition paper contained
It sits in the glove-box which is my escapades research and also doctrine
Tear it down-then in return build it back up
It is still intact yet I may add it is not defenseless against suffering sin
Yet I try to forget about the past and its downward succession
Vertigo locates my inner sinking self- as I feel as if roller coasting
Trying its best to create bogus oppression
Solitude vigorously knocks on my door attempting depression
I do although not answer back which in itself manifests as desperation
I firmly believe that it is a wicked foisting trick
Because the thought alone causes complete perspiration
Of the mind
Within me now and nearing my fragile soul
Creating body-ache and a weakness of thought
As an arrant-nearing its irregular physical toll
Hello-Goodbye mind that of an erupting volcano
Flush myself in absolution
That considered to be nearly mechanical as if drano
Henceforth-where the heck am I
My face gleams strangely with a smile
In submission I do not know where I stand-in attentive composition
Or am I in a state of denial
Could I be blistering lost and approaching a land of persistence
These roads all look the same
No landmarks or places of perception-I now feel an ethereal type consistence
Am I truly lost both in mind and geography
No more gas in tank-no more roads to find a path of destination
Am I writing the end to my own bibliography
Turn up the radio
And hear that anticipated sound
Will I panic- without bed sheets to huddle and hide within
I although decide not to beg or give in to the absurd
Another road-foot on the gas steadily with the environment passing so quick
Will I find what was never as of yet considered
A joy ride such as this has turned into a load
A burden
A crazy strain
It all adds up
To a debilitating brain drain
I keep driving with fuel nearly deplete
A simple prayer of home
Is what would make me complete

WRITTEN BY: BRIAN MOILANEN

Made in the USA
San Bernardino, CA
21 January 2015